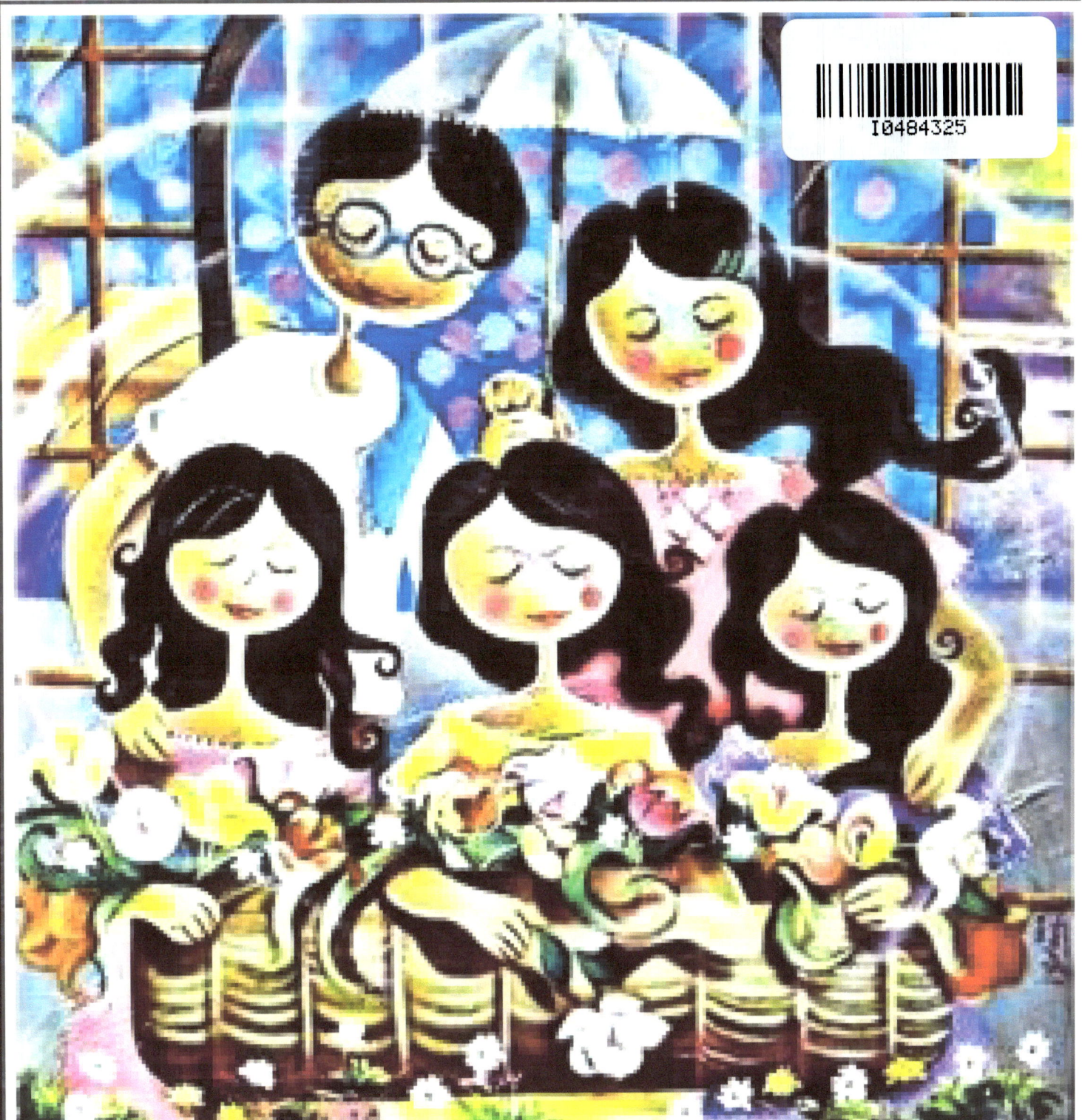

Joeyboi Galang - Growing Up Together, 30x30 in. Acrylic

WELCOME! We hope you will enjoy this Art Gallery Book of collection of paintings and artwork by JOEYBOI GALANG. His actual paintings are available in Philippines and can be ordered in person or by mail or online. He can accept commission works. He can be contacted thru his facebook account under his name. Or contact the publisher. Meanwhile, this book is size 8.5x11 inches. Each page is a paper print of his paintings and can cut out and framed separately, suitable for wall decor. The whole book is suitable as coffee table book for display in your living room and perfect as conversation piece.

Self-Published by Tatay Jobo Elizes. Printed in USA. ISBN-13: 978-1503016668 & ISBN-10: 1503016668
Other Tatay books are shown in http://tinyurl.com/mj76ccq & www.jobelizes.webs.com
Contact email: job_elizes@yahoo.com

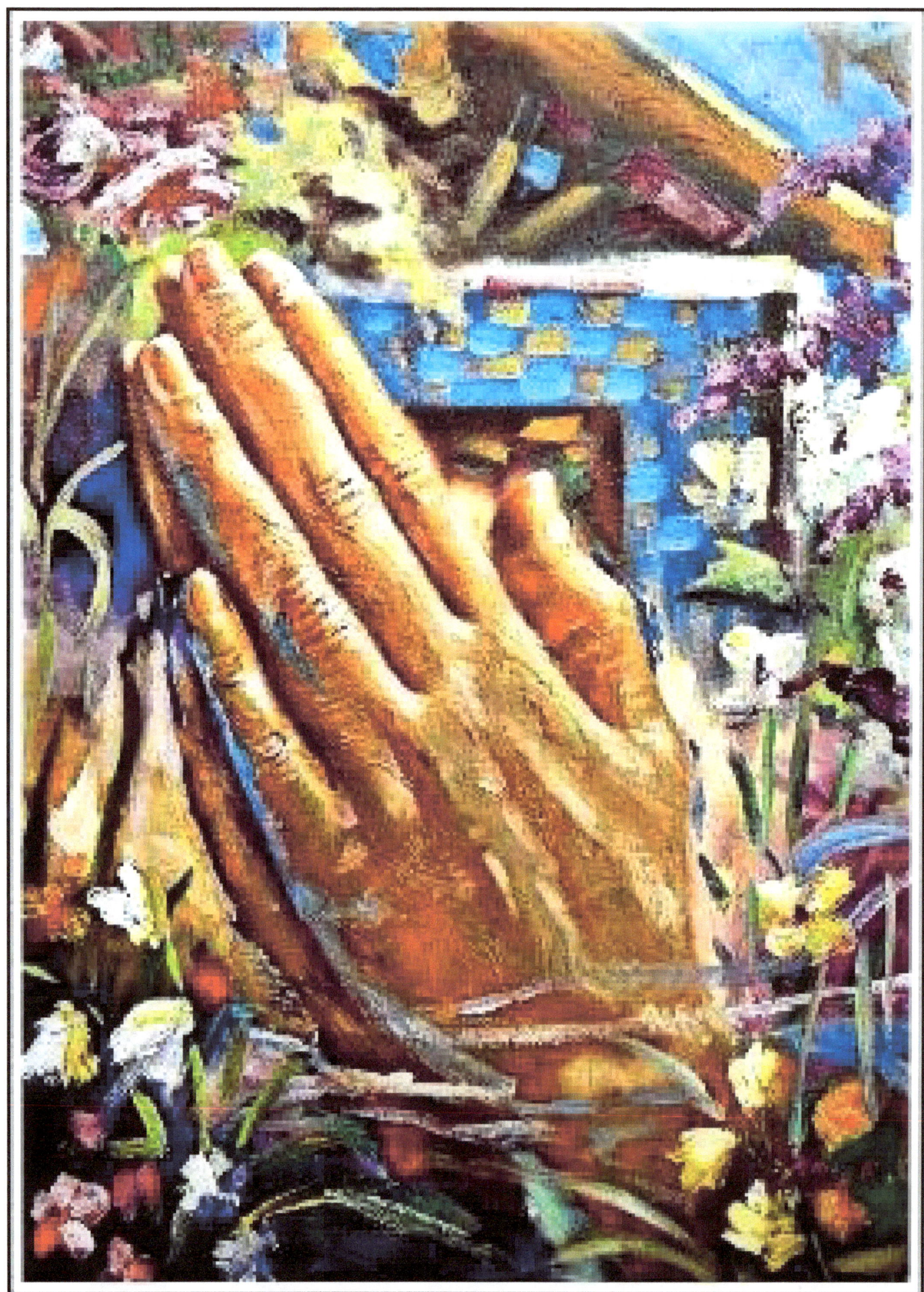

Joeyboi Galang - My Prayers, 18x24 in. Oil

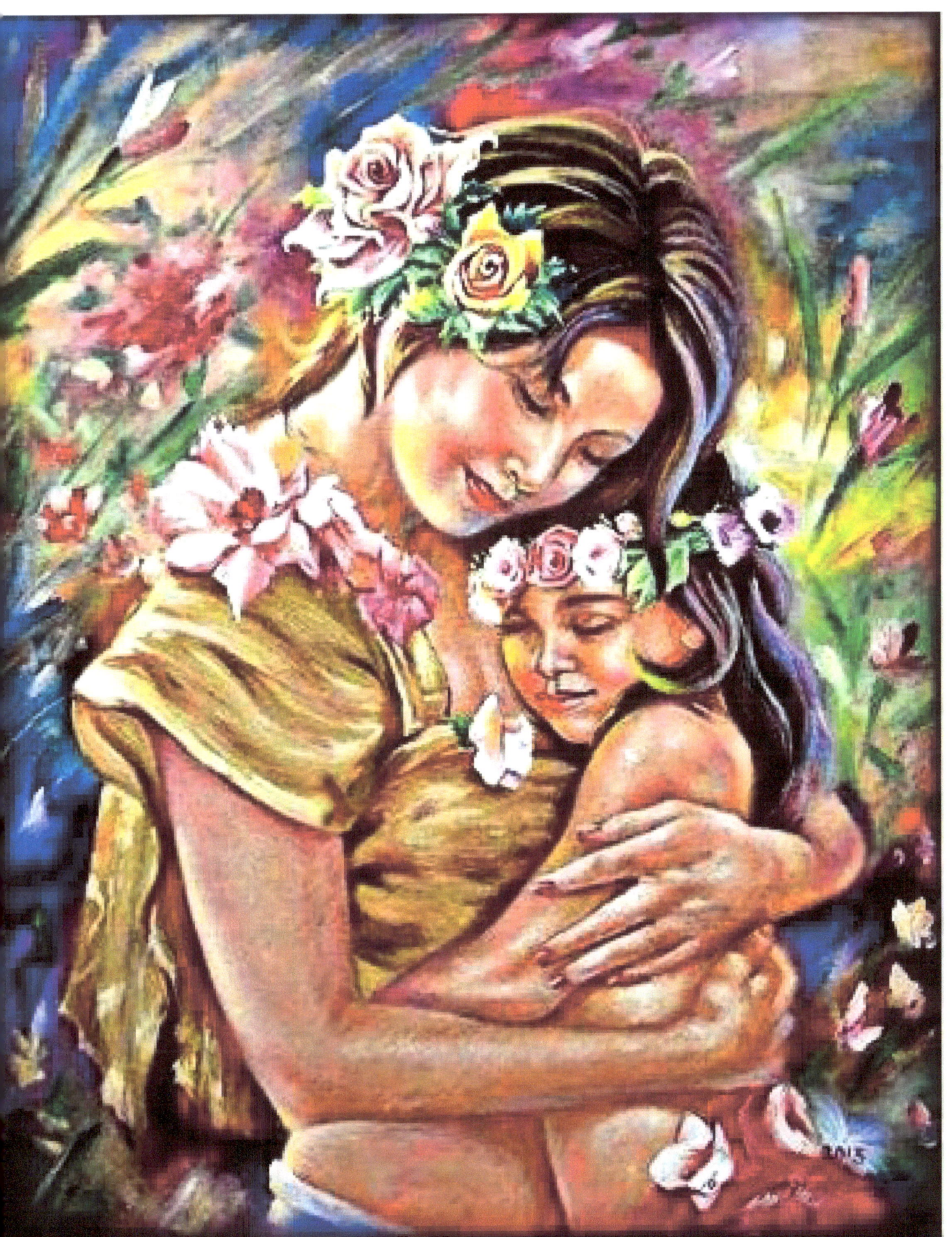

Joeyboi Galang - Hug So Tight, 14x30 in. Oil

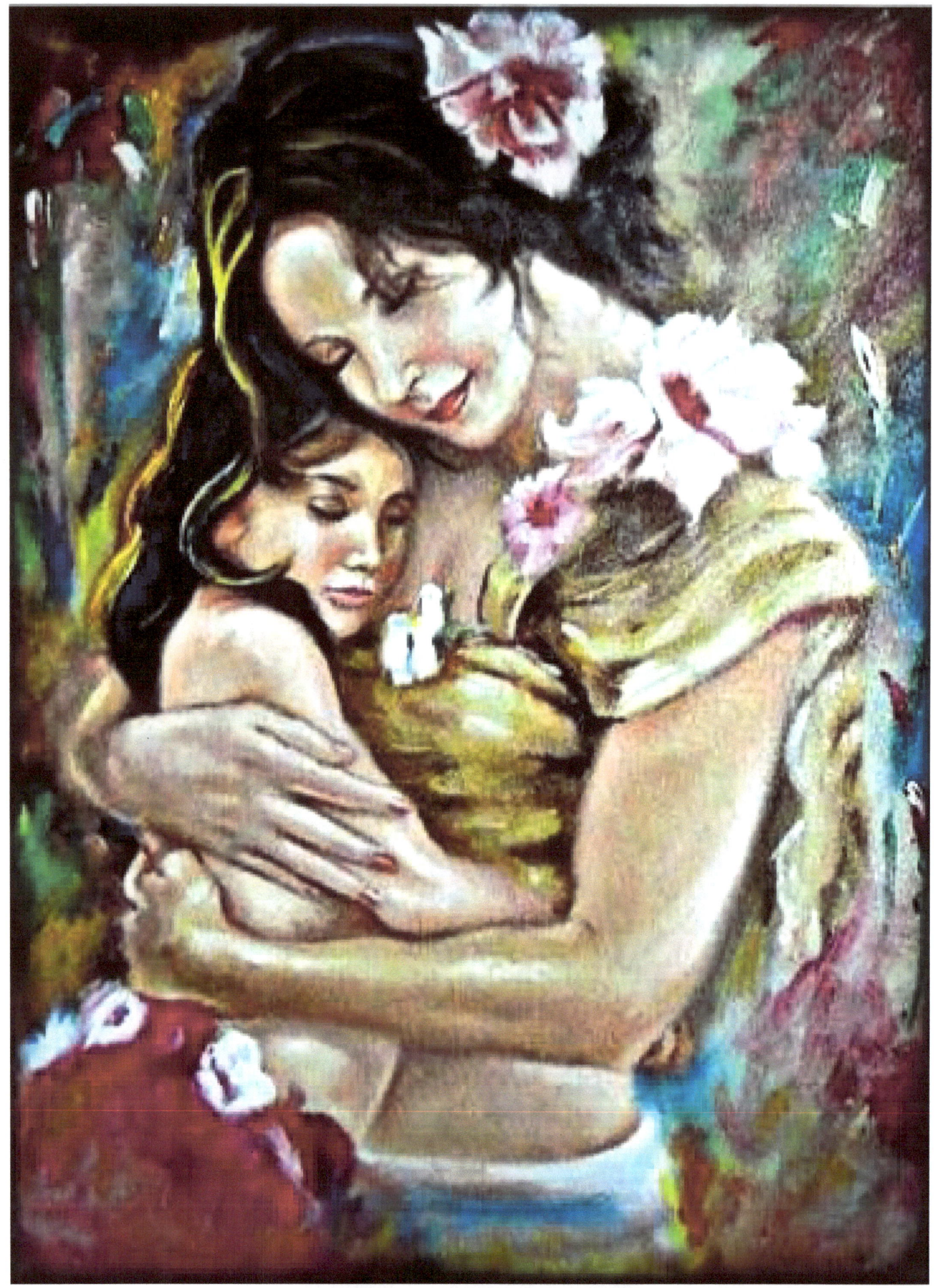

Joeyboi Galang - Yakap Higpit, 18x24 in. Oil

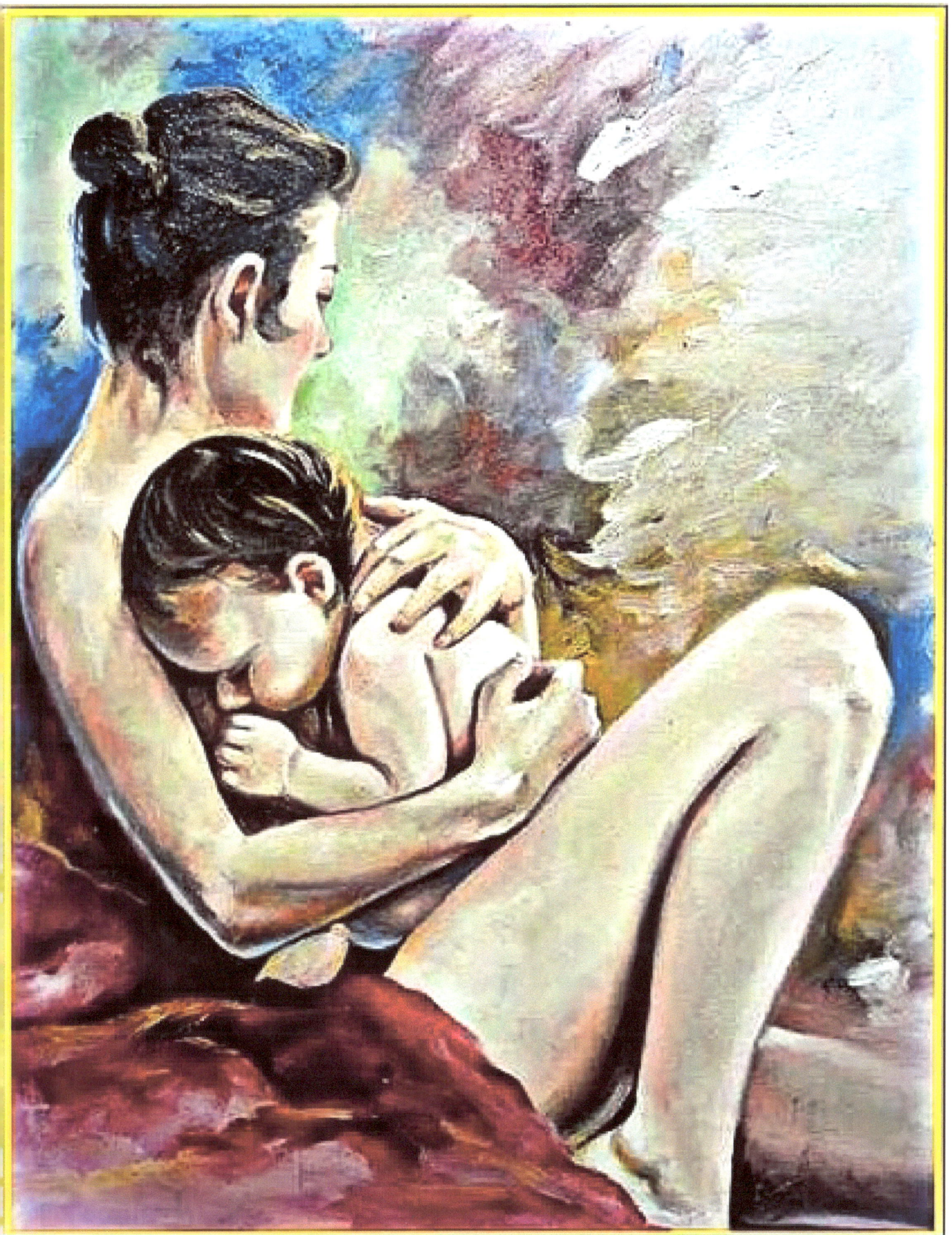

Joeyboi Galang - Mother's Child, 18x24 in. Oil

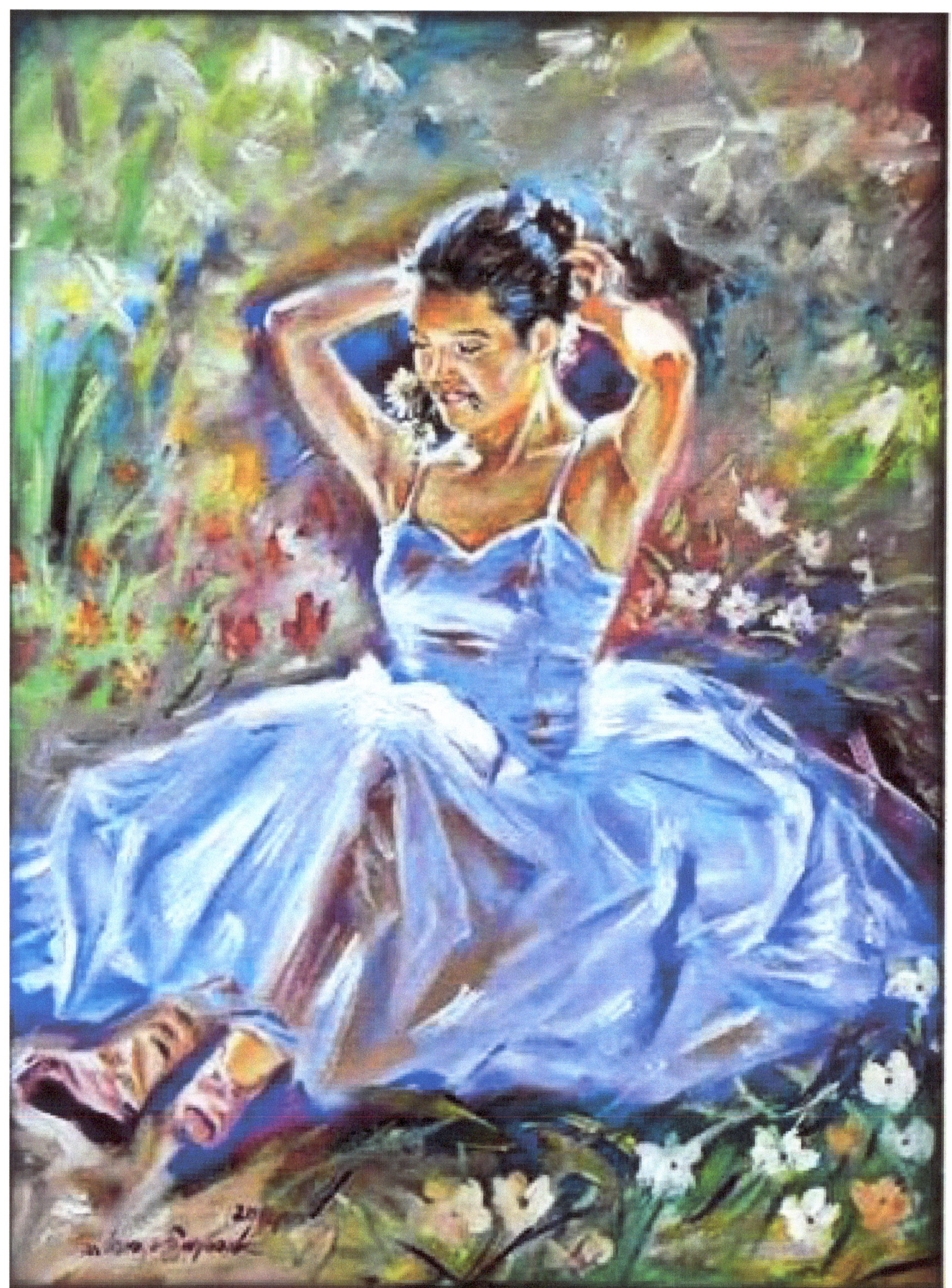

Joeyboi Galang - Victorian Ballerina, 18x24 in. Oil

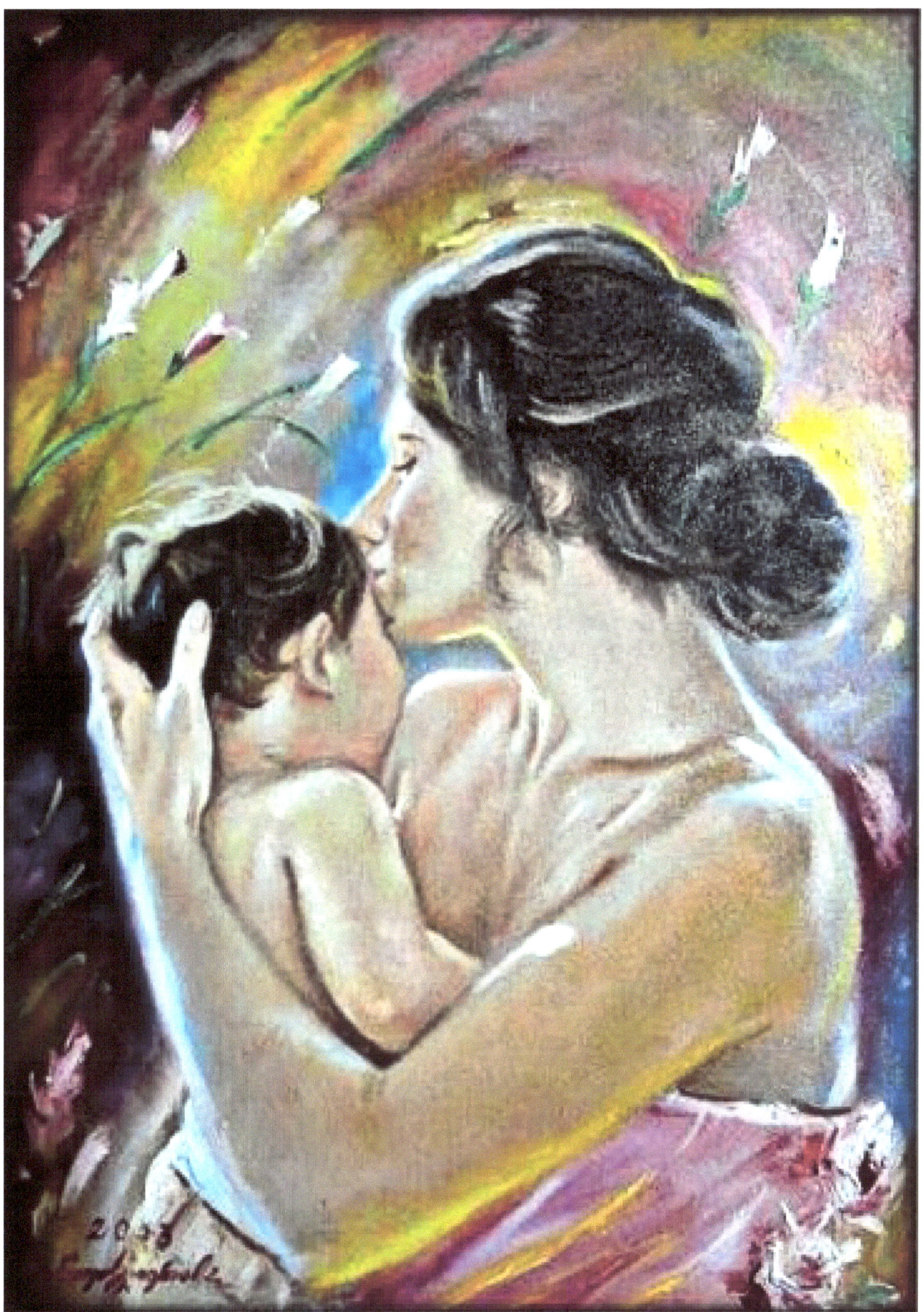

Joeyboi Galang - Lab Lab Kit Kit, 18x24 in. Oil

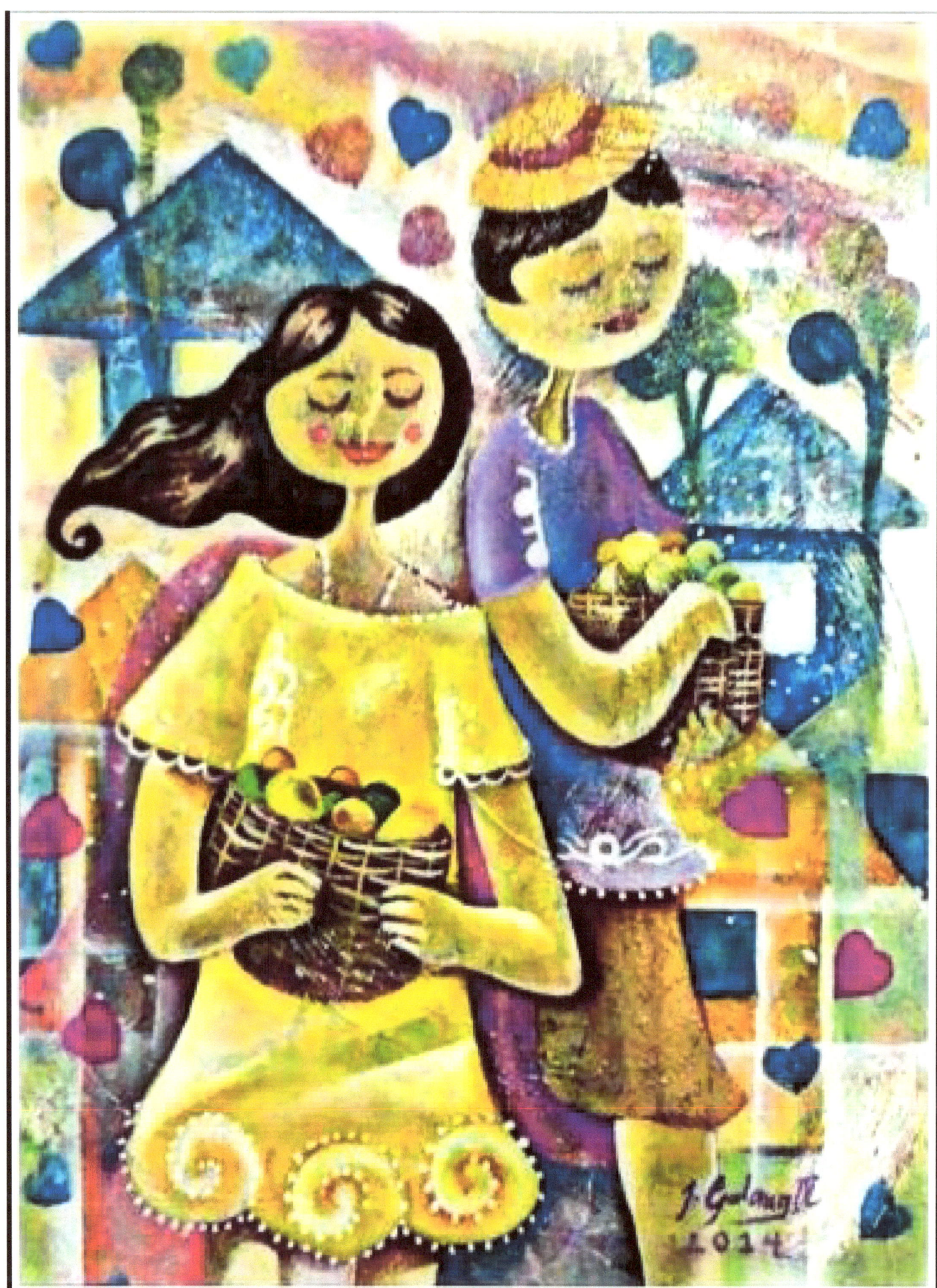

Joeyboi Galang - Fruits For Everyone, 18x24 in. Acrylic

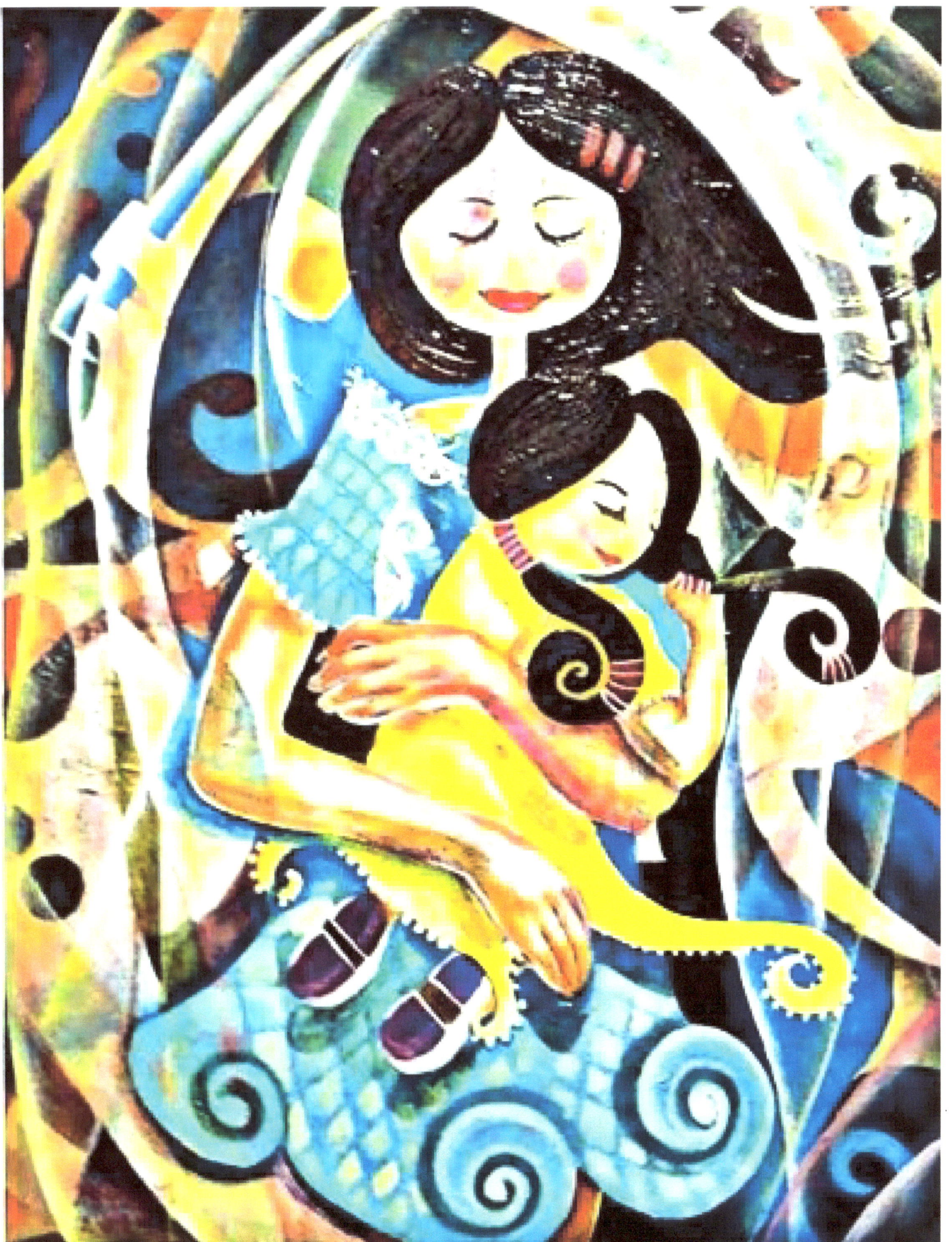

Joeyboi Galang - Warm Embrace, 24x30 in Acrylic

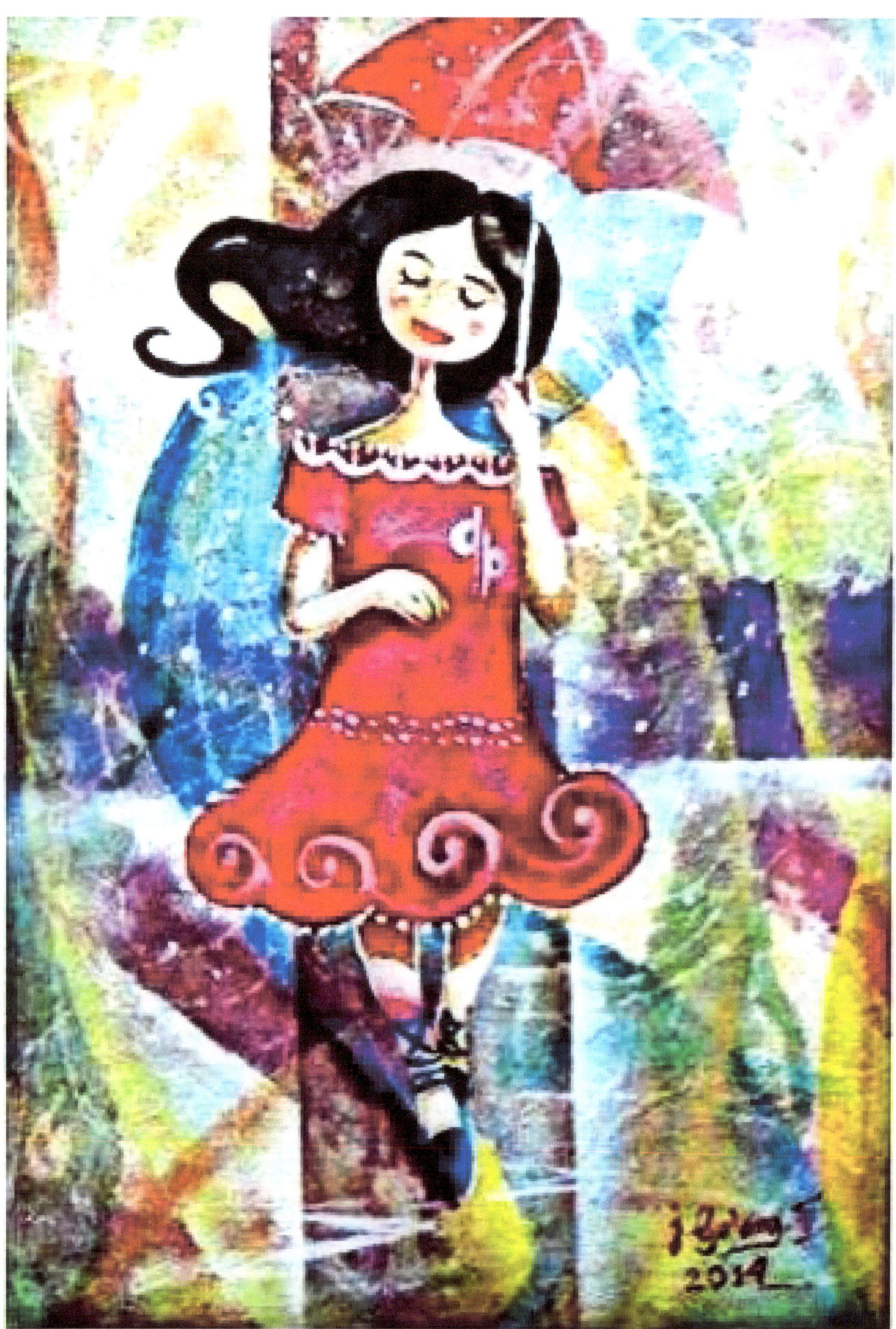

Joeyboi Galang - Color Of The Day, 12x16 in. Acrylic

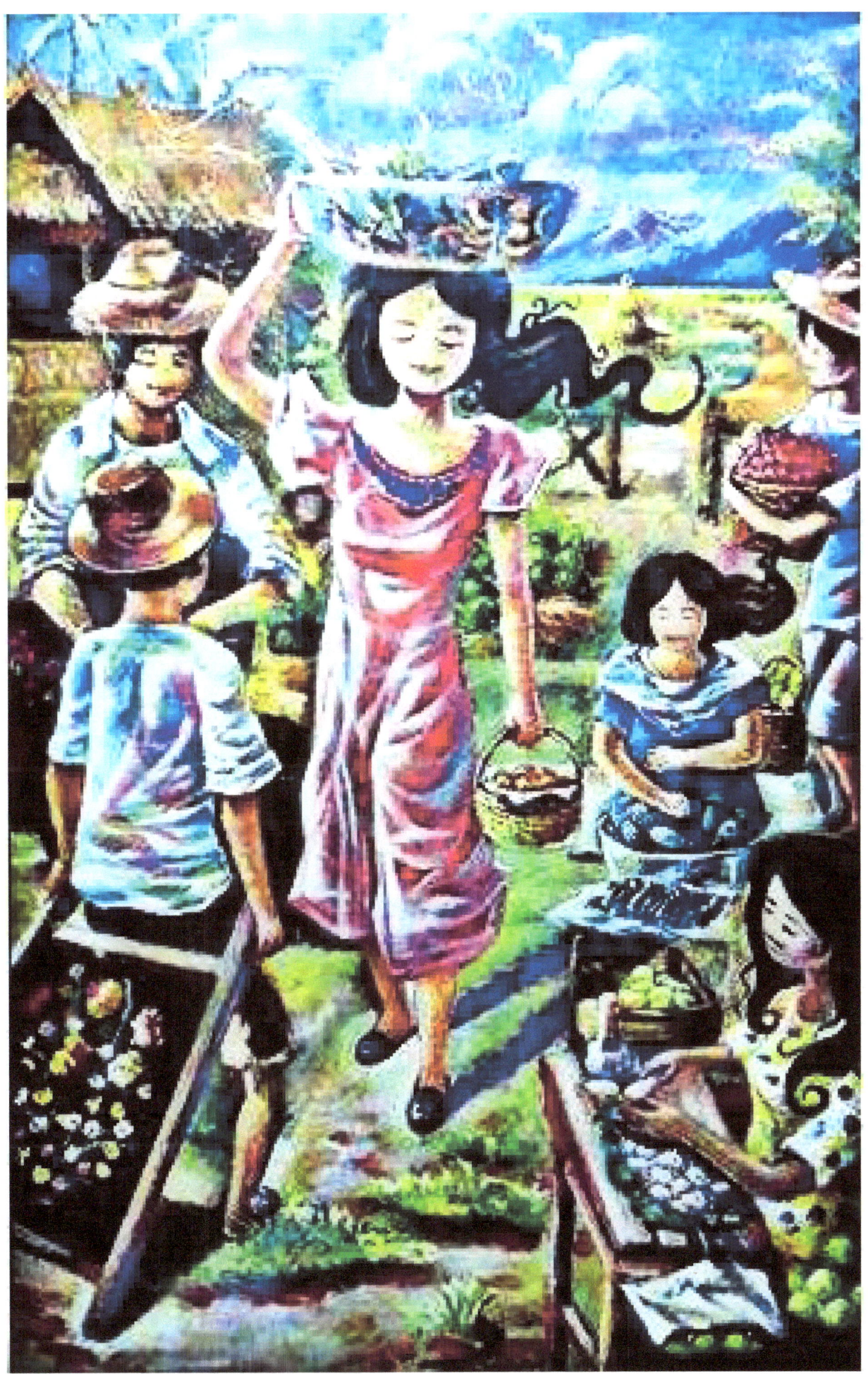

Joeyboi Galang - Untitled

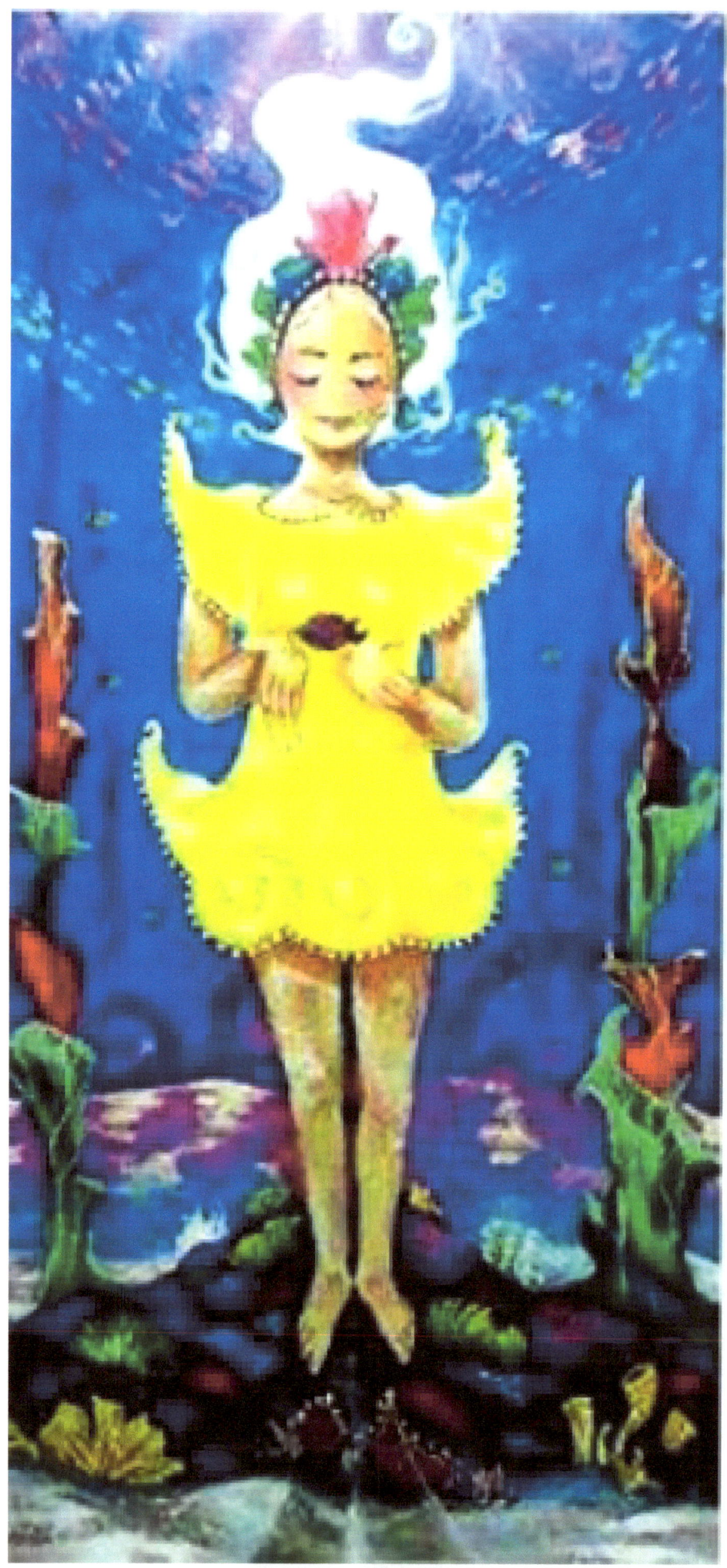

Joeyboi Galang - Untitled

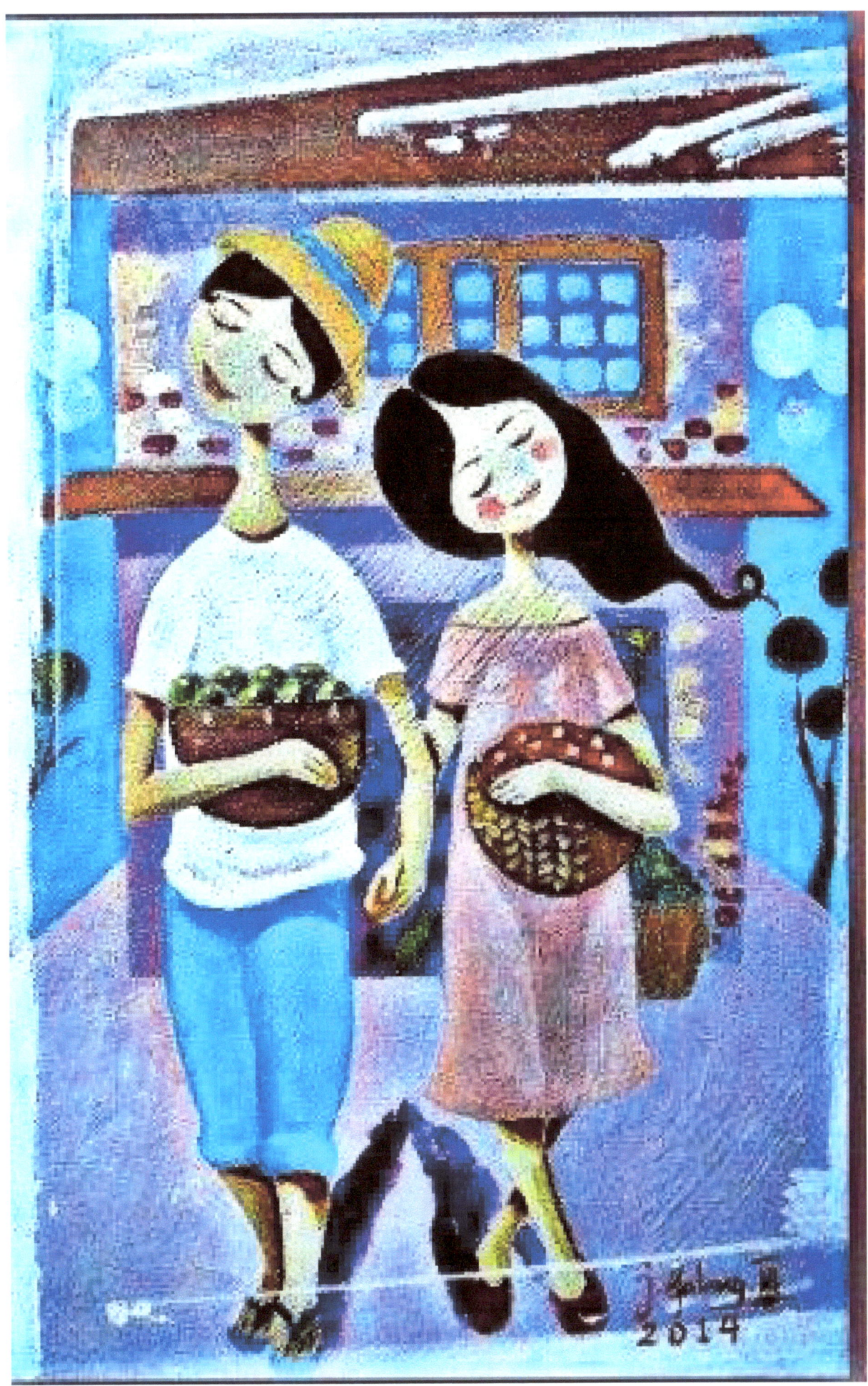

Joeyboi Galang - Untitled, 2014

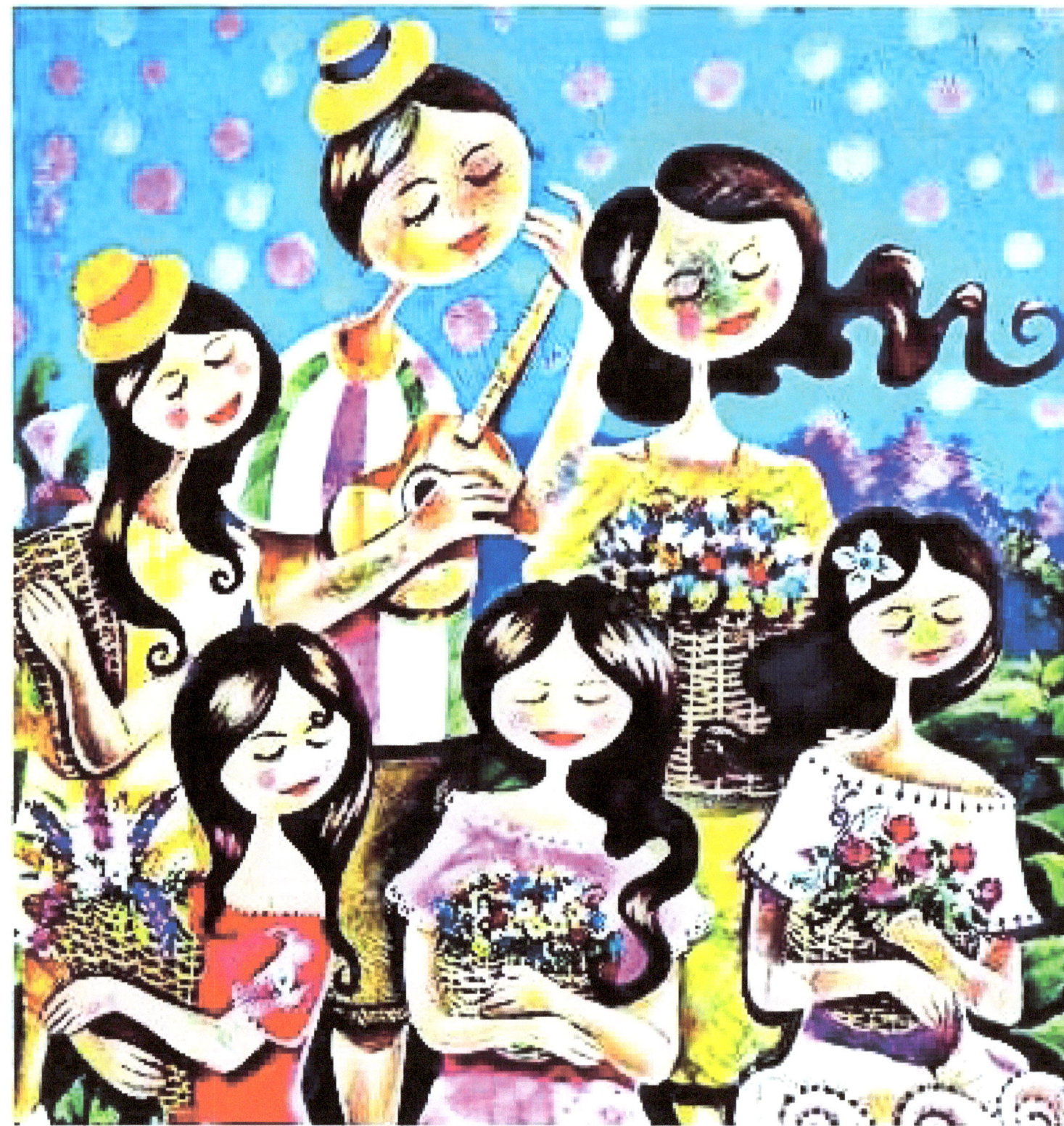

Joeyboi Galang - Family Bound by Love, 30x30 in. Acrylic

WELCOME! We hope you will enjoy this Art Gallery Book of collection of paintings and artwork by JOEYBOI GALANG. His actual paintings are available in Philippines and can be ordered in person or by mail or online. He can accept commission works. He can be contacted thru his facebook account under his name. Meanwhile, this book is size 8.5x11 inches. Each page is a paper print of his paintings and can cut out and framed separately, suitable for wall decor. The whole book is suitable as coffee table book for display in your living room and perfect as conversation piece.

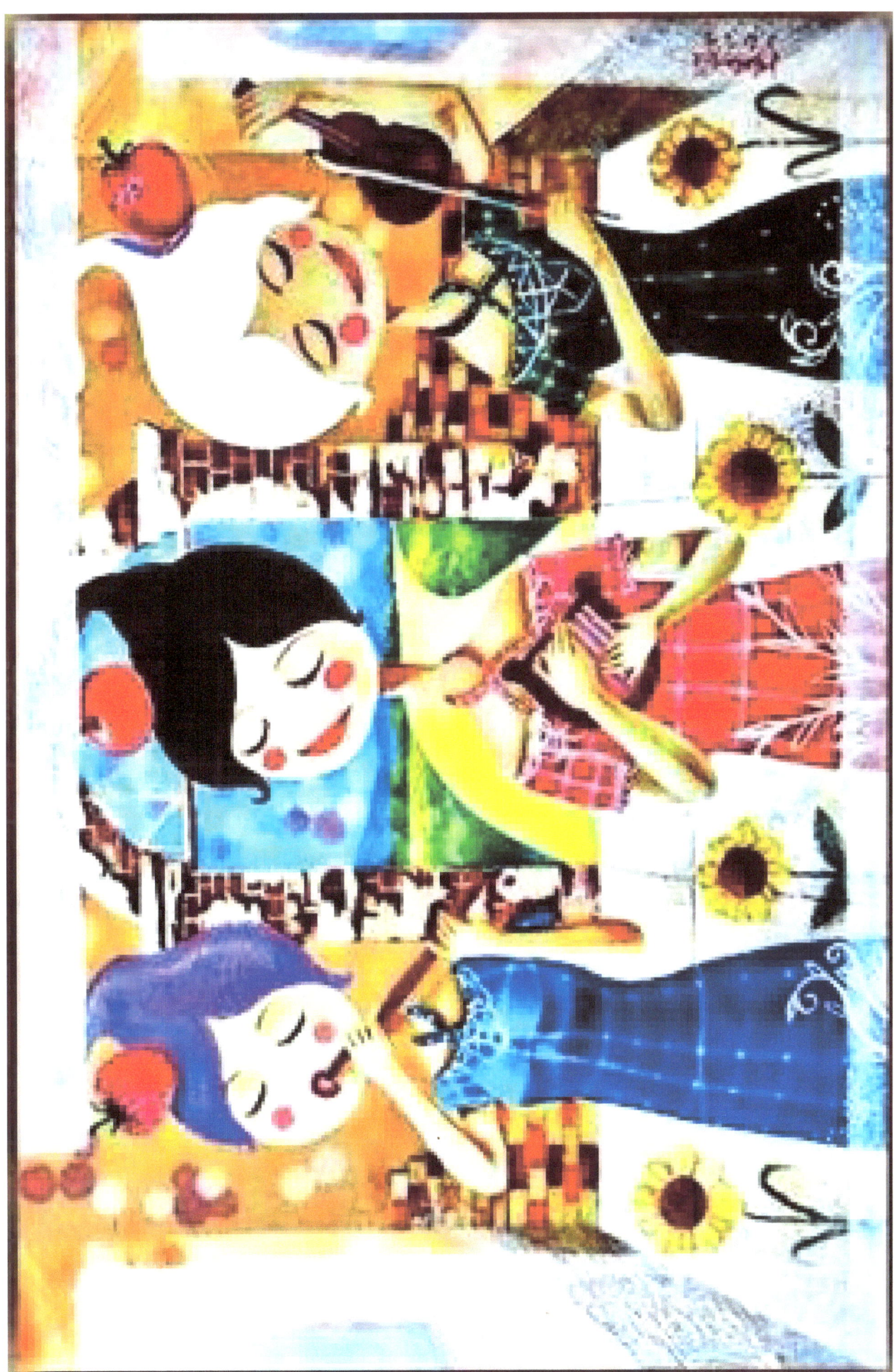

Joeyboi Galang - Untitled

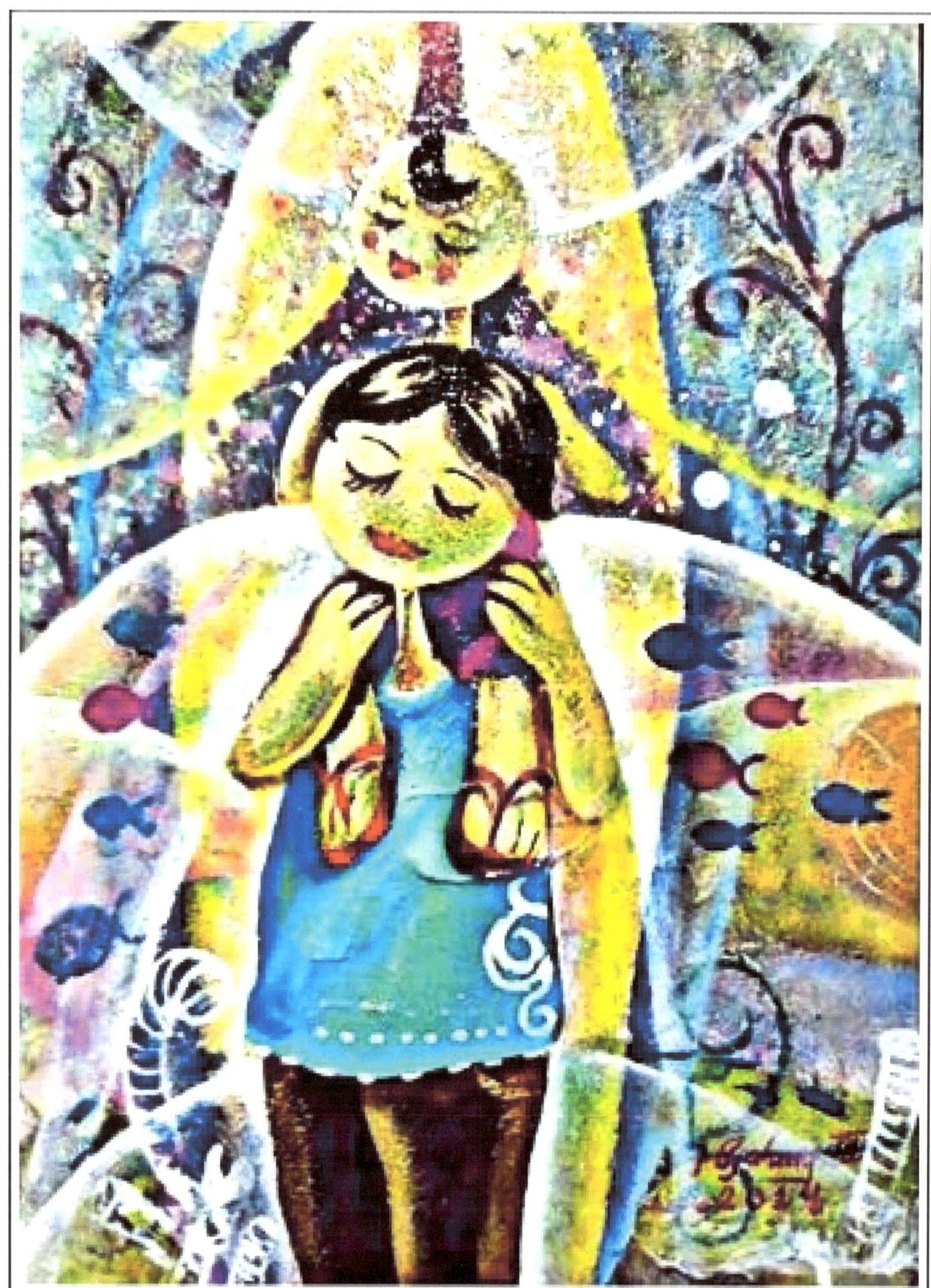

Joeyboi Galang - Daddy's Boy, 18x24 in. Acrylic

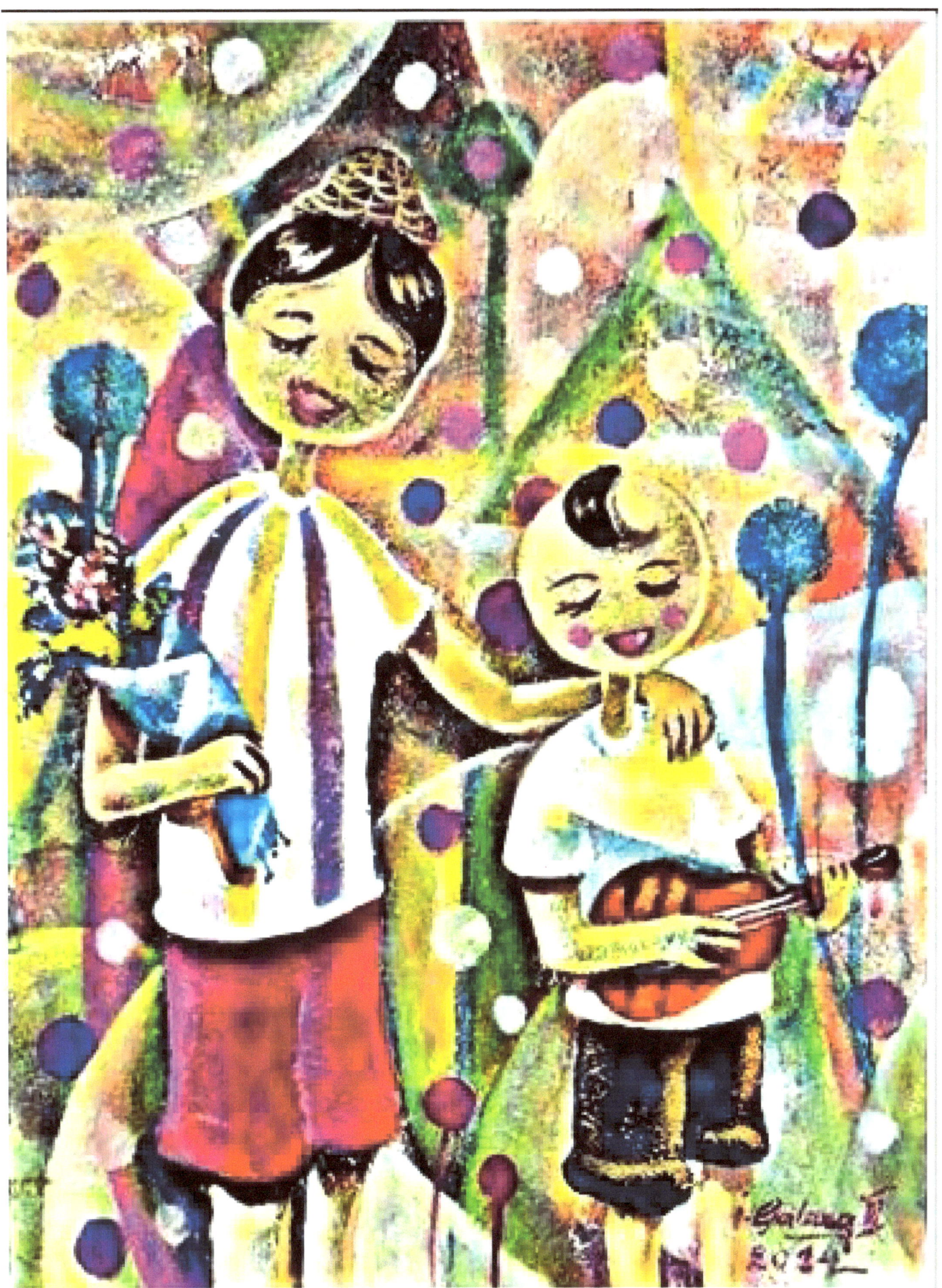

Joeyboi Galang - The Suitors, 18x24 in. Acrylic

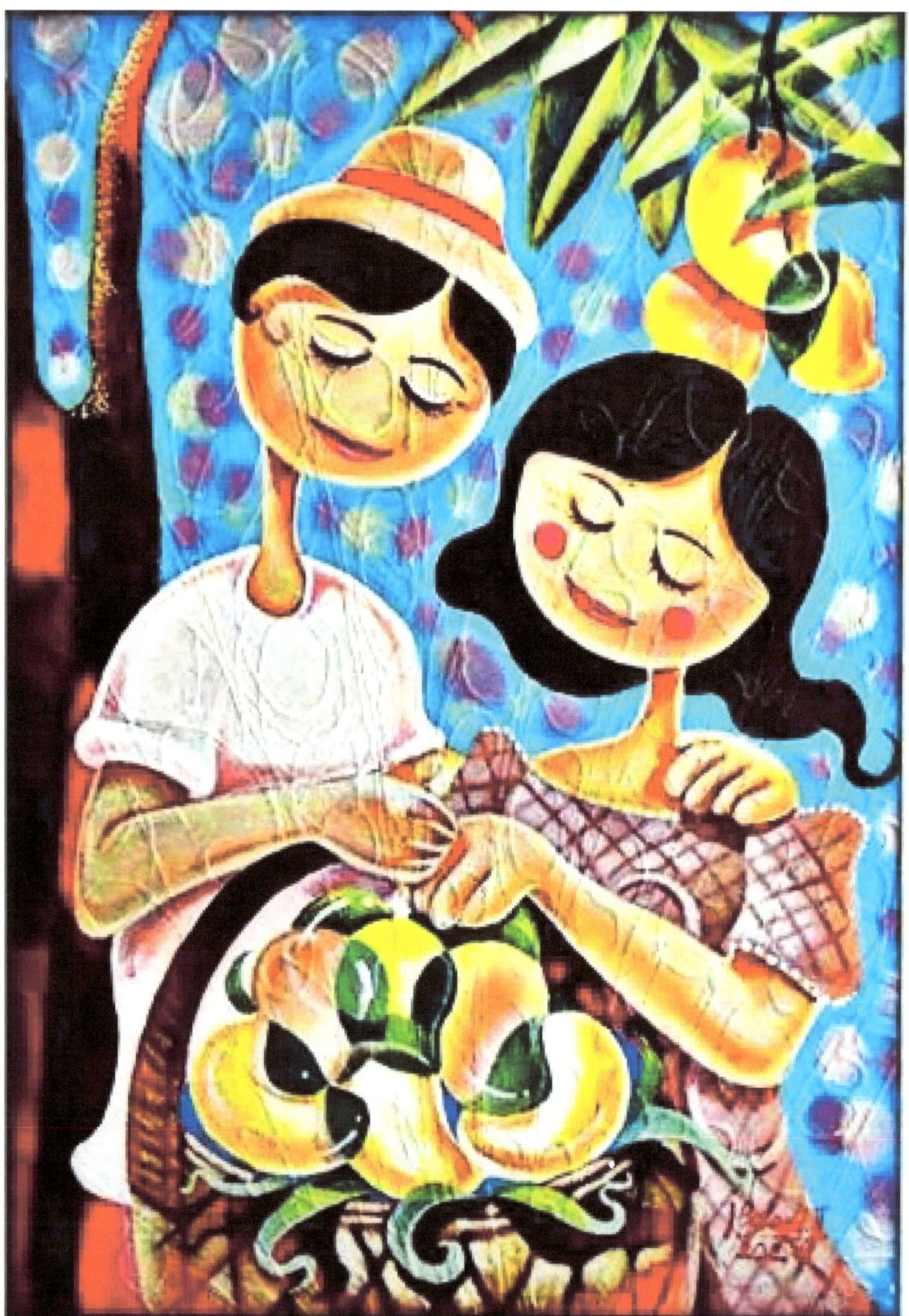

Joeyboi Galang - Harvest Delight, 19x26 in. Acrylic

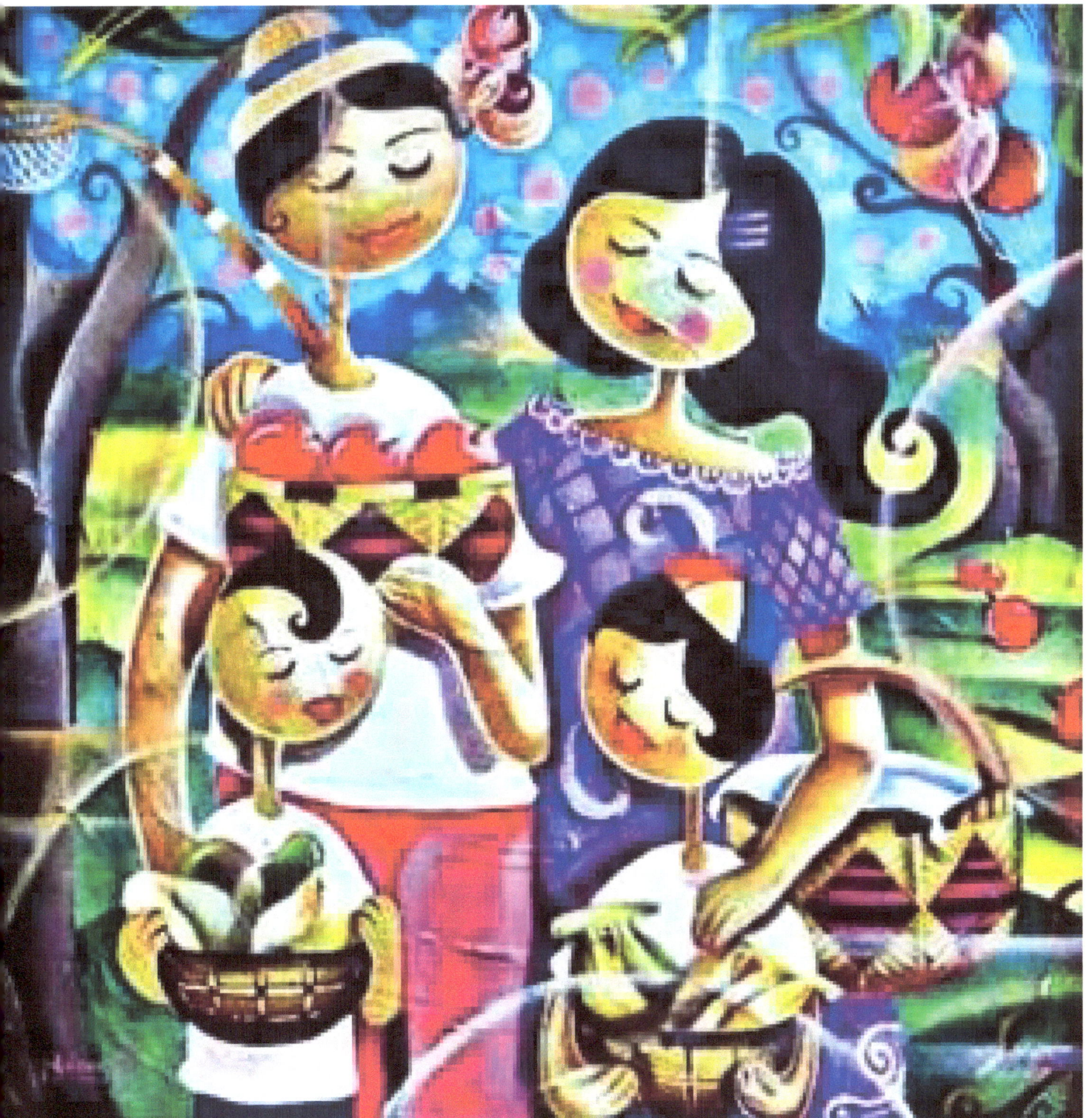

Joeyboi Galang - Fruit of Dreams, 30x30 in. Acrylic

WELCOME! We hope you will enjoy this Art Gallery Book of collection of paintings and artwork by JOEYBOI GALANG. His actual paintings are available in Philippines and can be ordered in person or by mail or online. He can accept commission works. He can be contacted thru his facebook account under his name. Meanwhile, this book is size 8.5x11 inches. Each page is a paper print of his paintings and can cut out and framed separately, suitable for wall decor. The whole book is suitable as coffee table book for display in your living room and perfect as conversation piece.

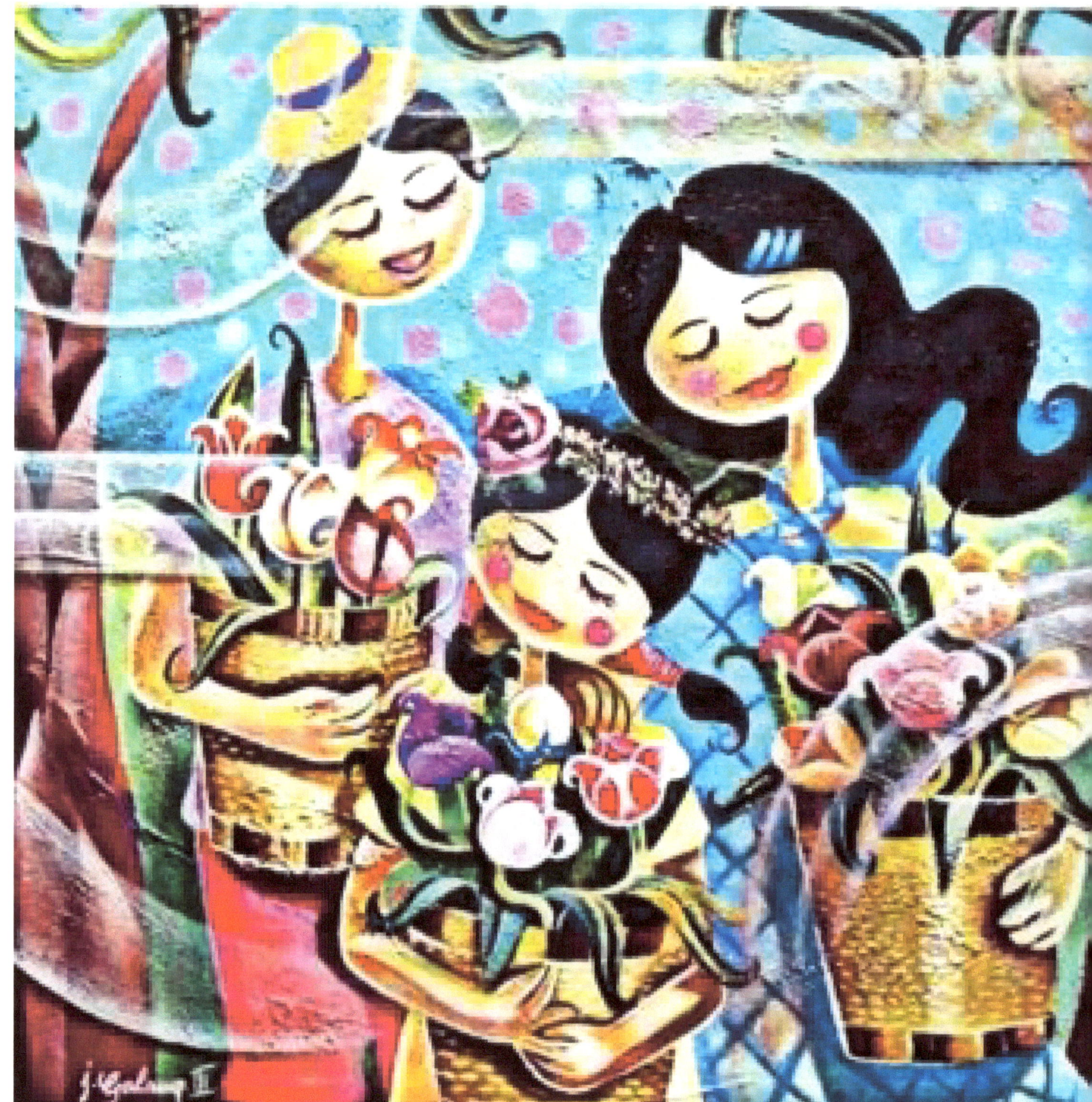

Joeyboi Galang - Basket Full of Love, 30x30 in. Acrylic

WELCOME! We hope you will enjoy this Art Gallery Book of collection of paintings and artwork by JOEYBOI GALANG. His actual paintings are available in Philippines and can be ordered in person or by mail or online. He can accept commission works. He can be contacted thru his facebook account under his name. Meanwhile, this book is size 8.5x11 inches. Each page is a paper print of his paintings and can cut out and framed separately, suitable for wall decor. The whole book is suitable as coffee table book for display in your living room and perfect as conversation piece.

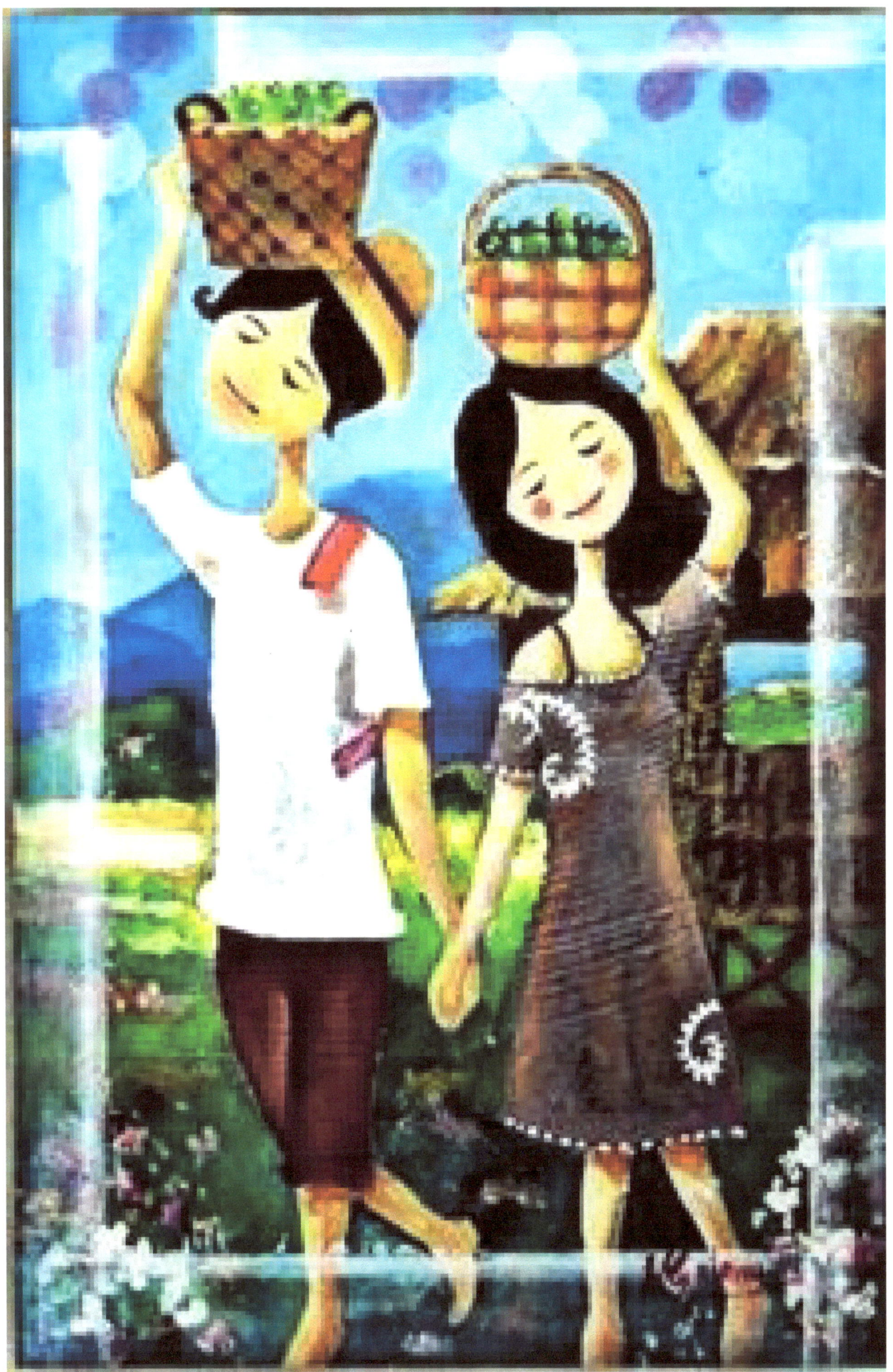

Joeyboi Galang - All Things Grow Better With Love, 12x18 in. Acrylic

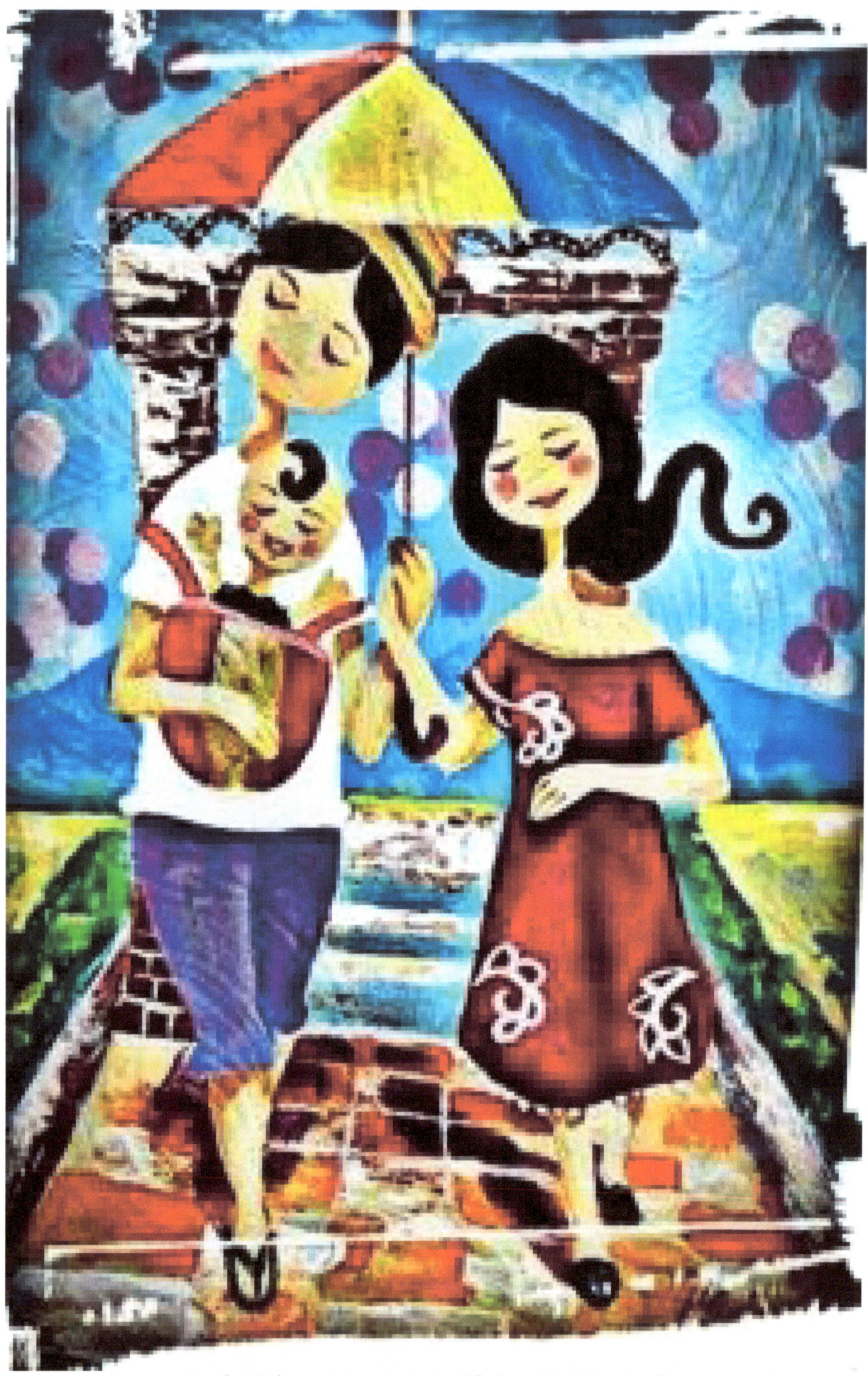

Joeyboi Galang - A Love to Last a Lifetime, 13x19 in. Acrylic

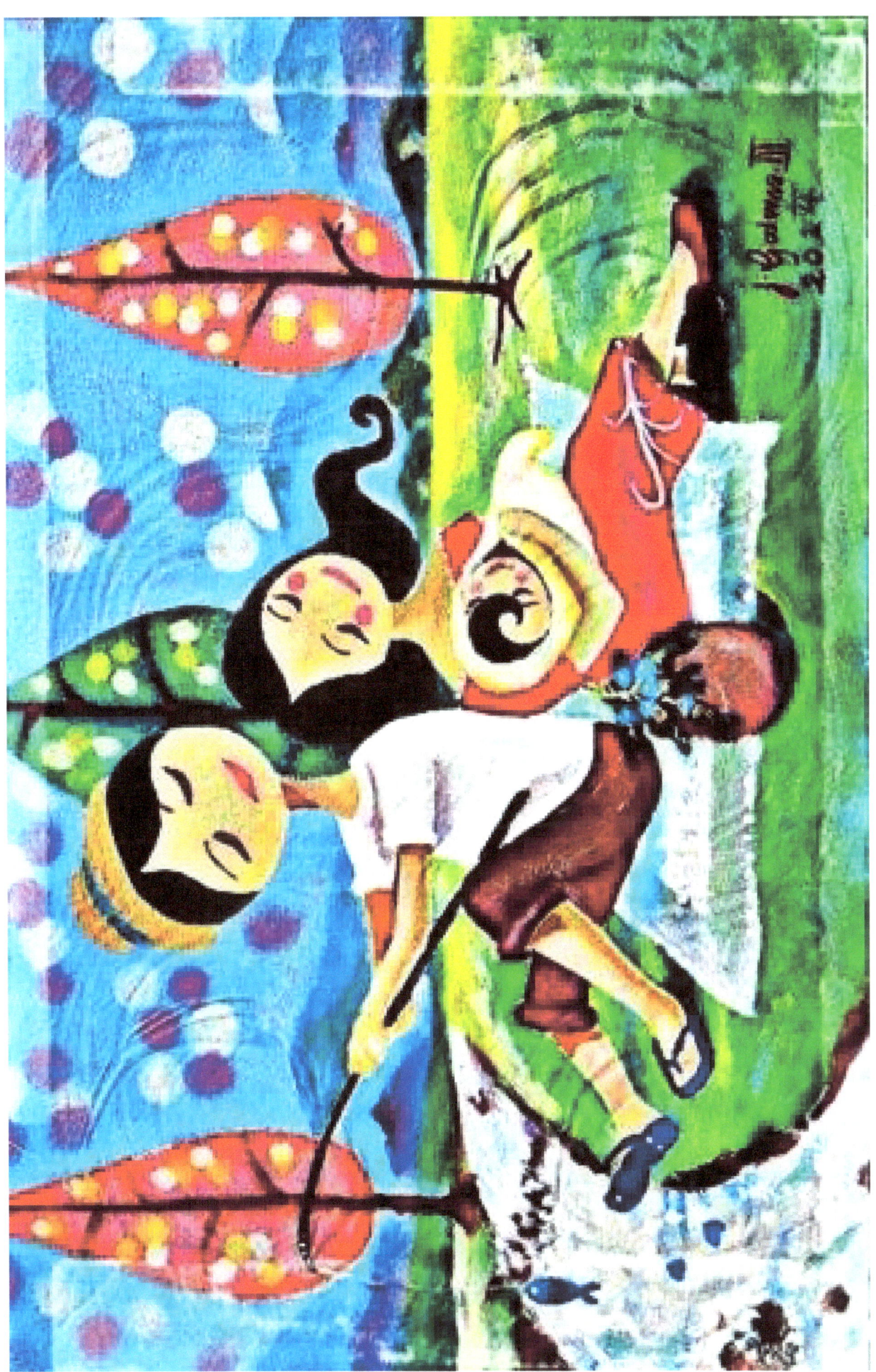

Joeyboi Galang - The Catch of the Day, 12x18 in. Acrylic

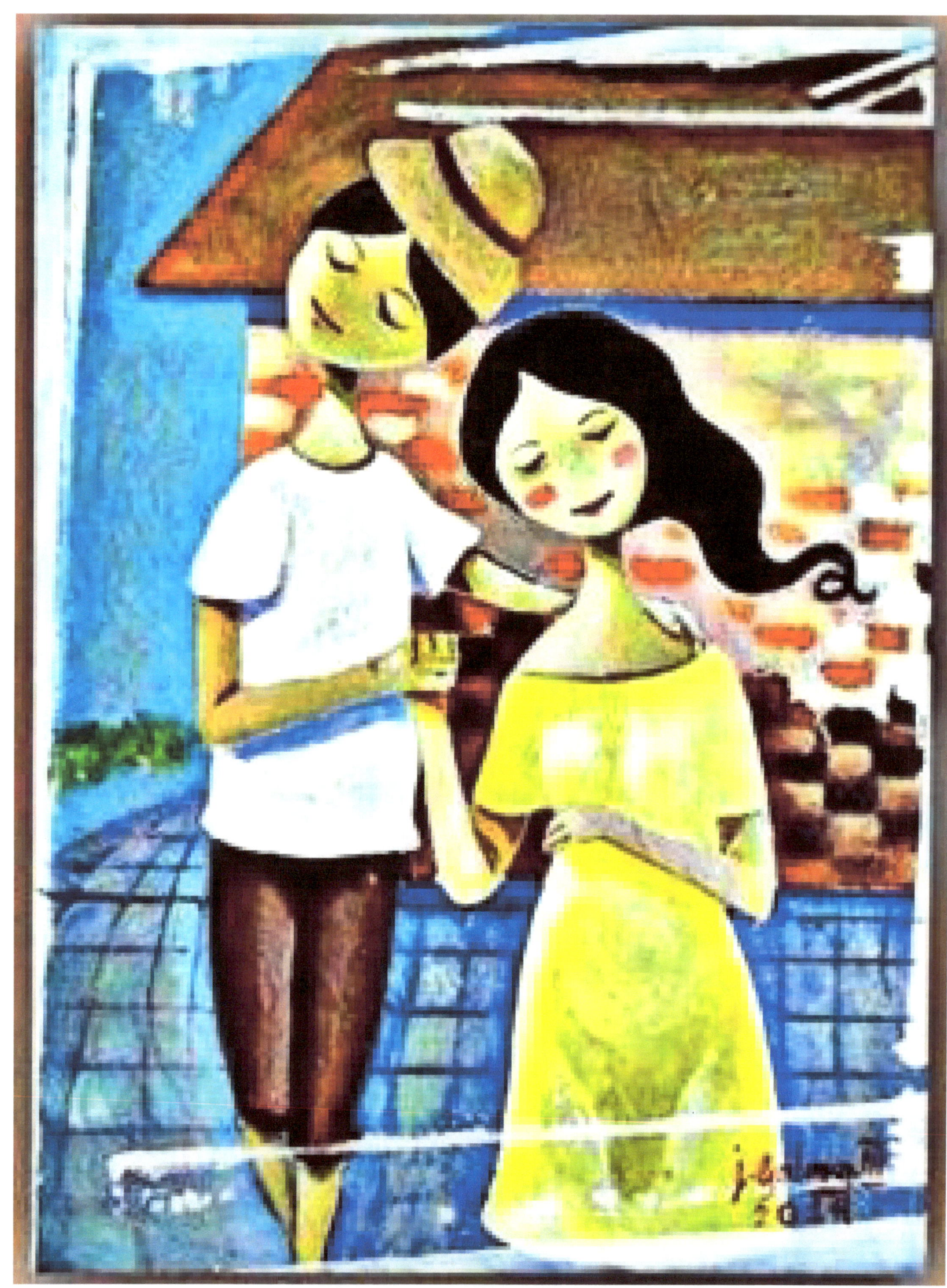

Joeyboi Galang - New Hope, 12x16 in. Acrylic

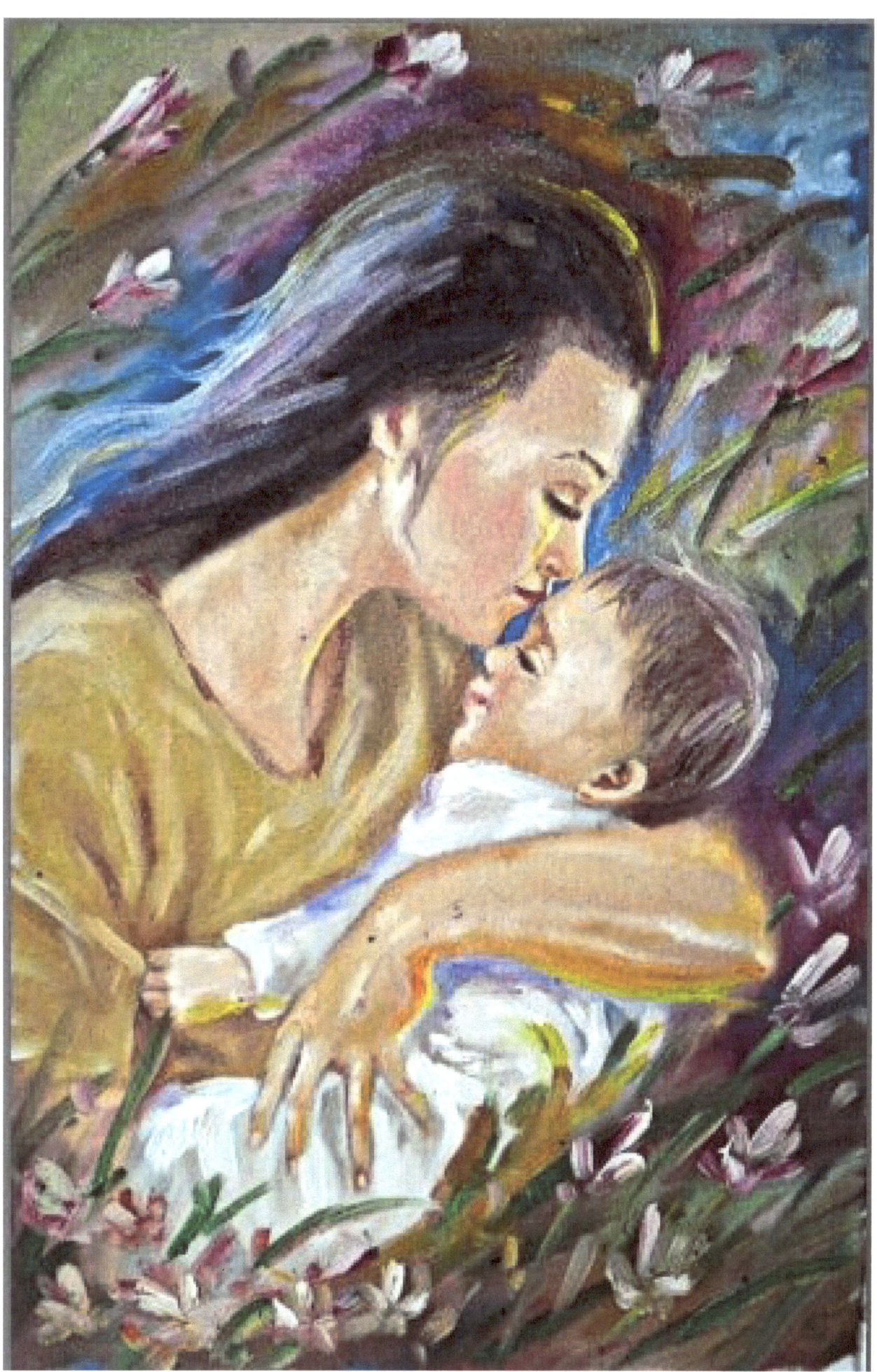

Joeyboi Galang - Untitled

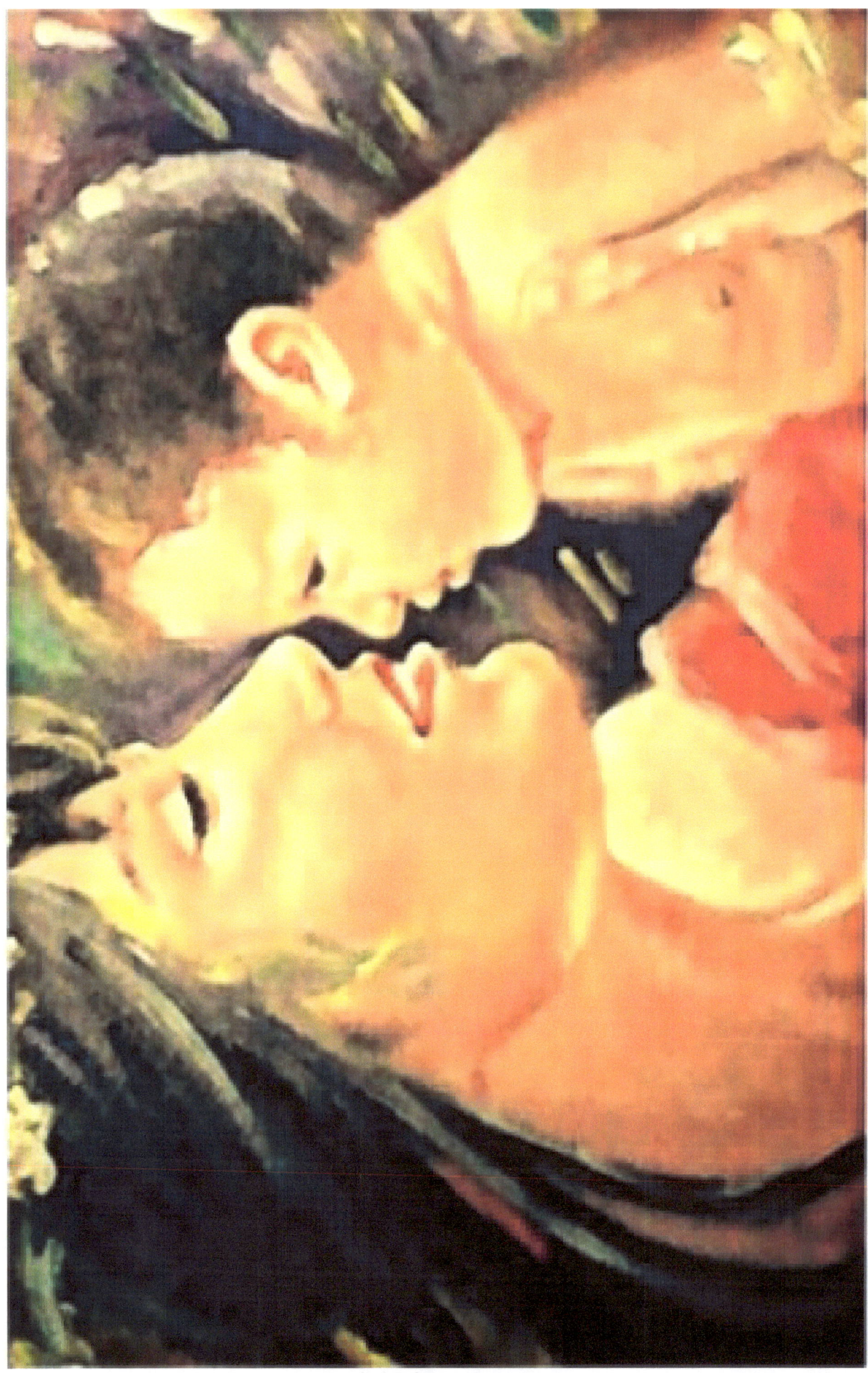

Joeyboi Galang - First Love

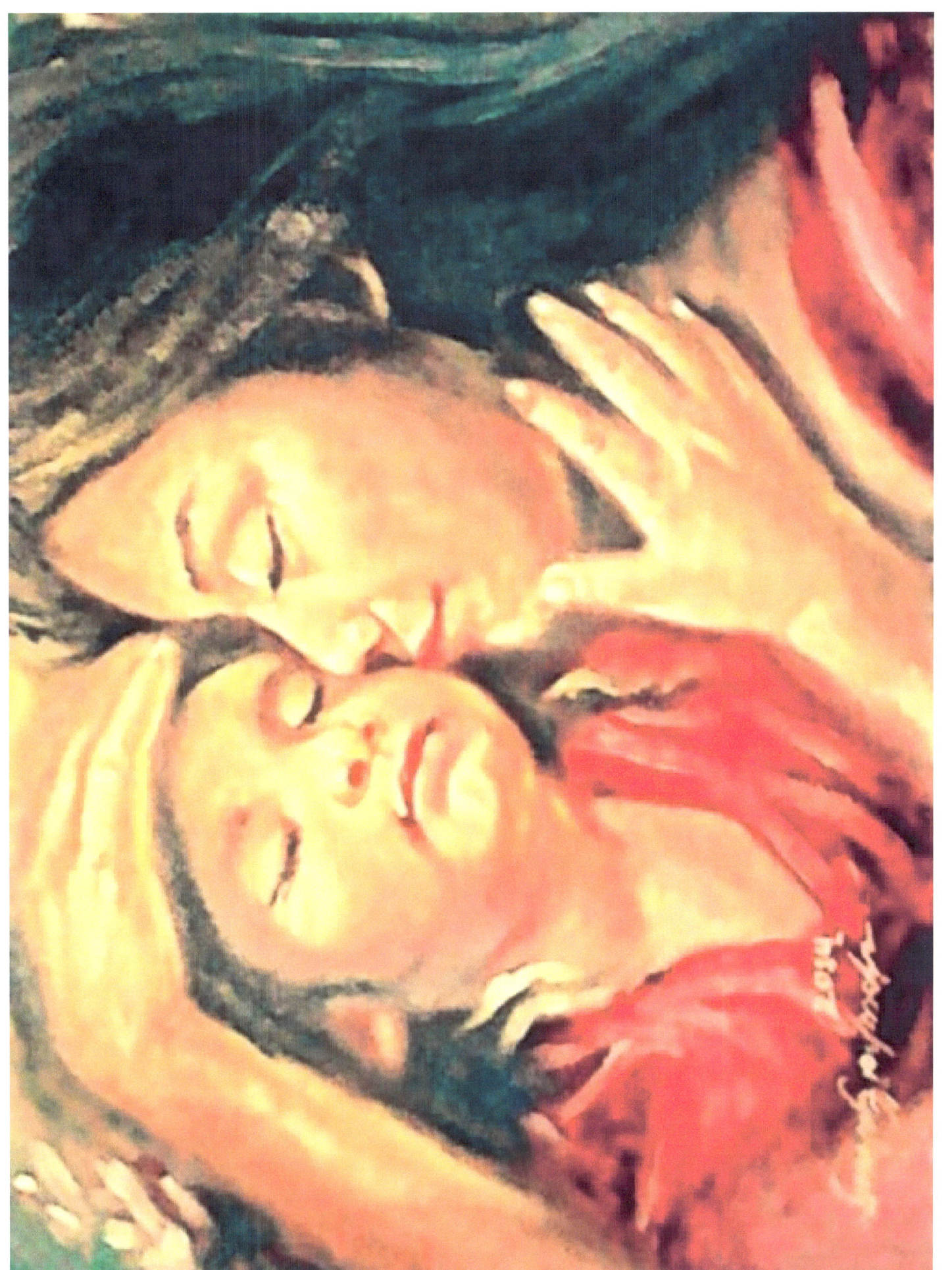

Joeyboi Galang - Untitled

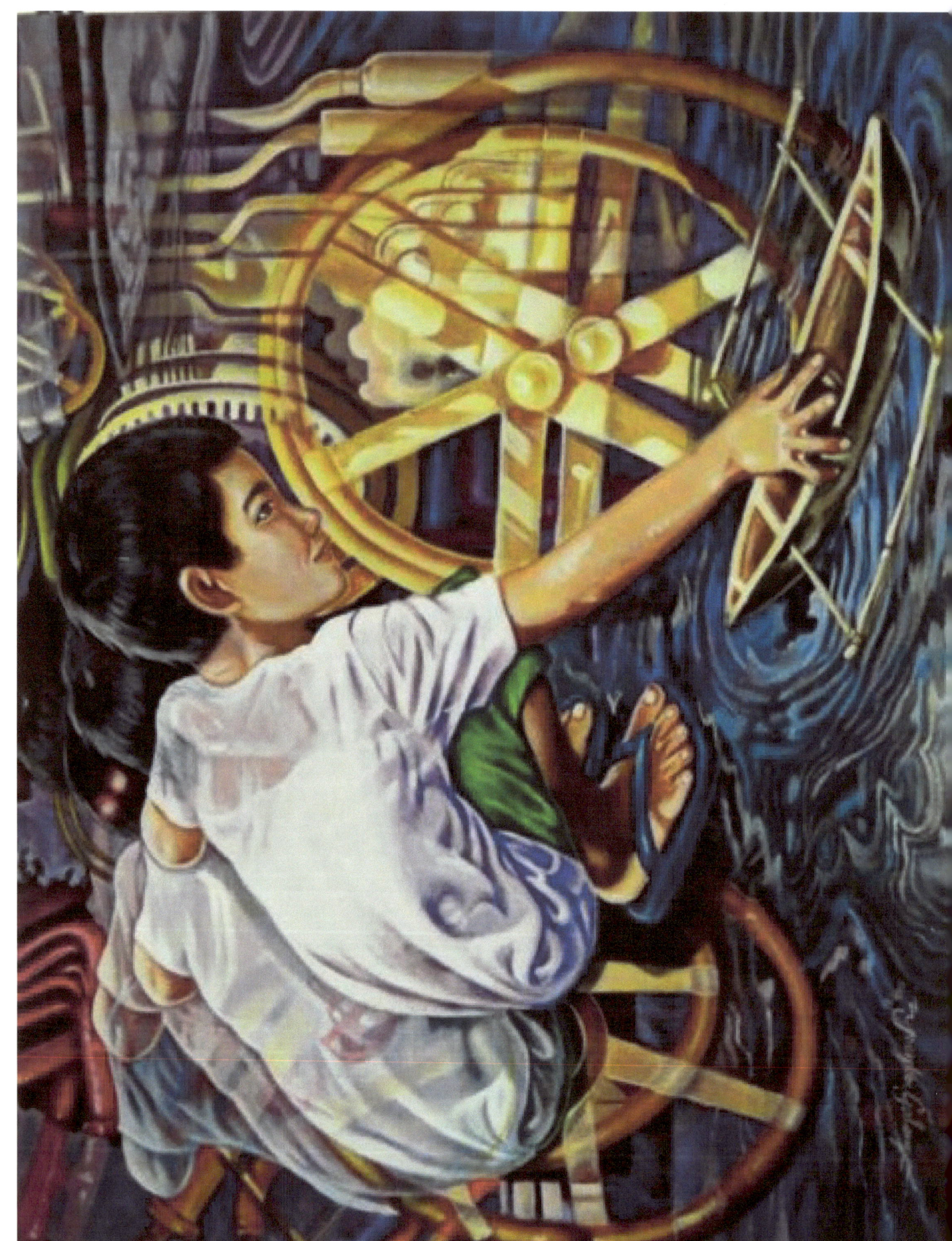

Joeyboi Galang - Untitled

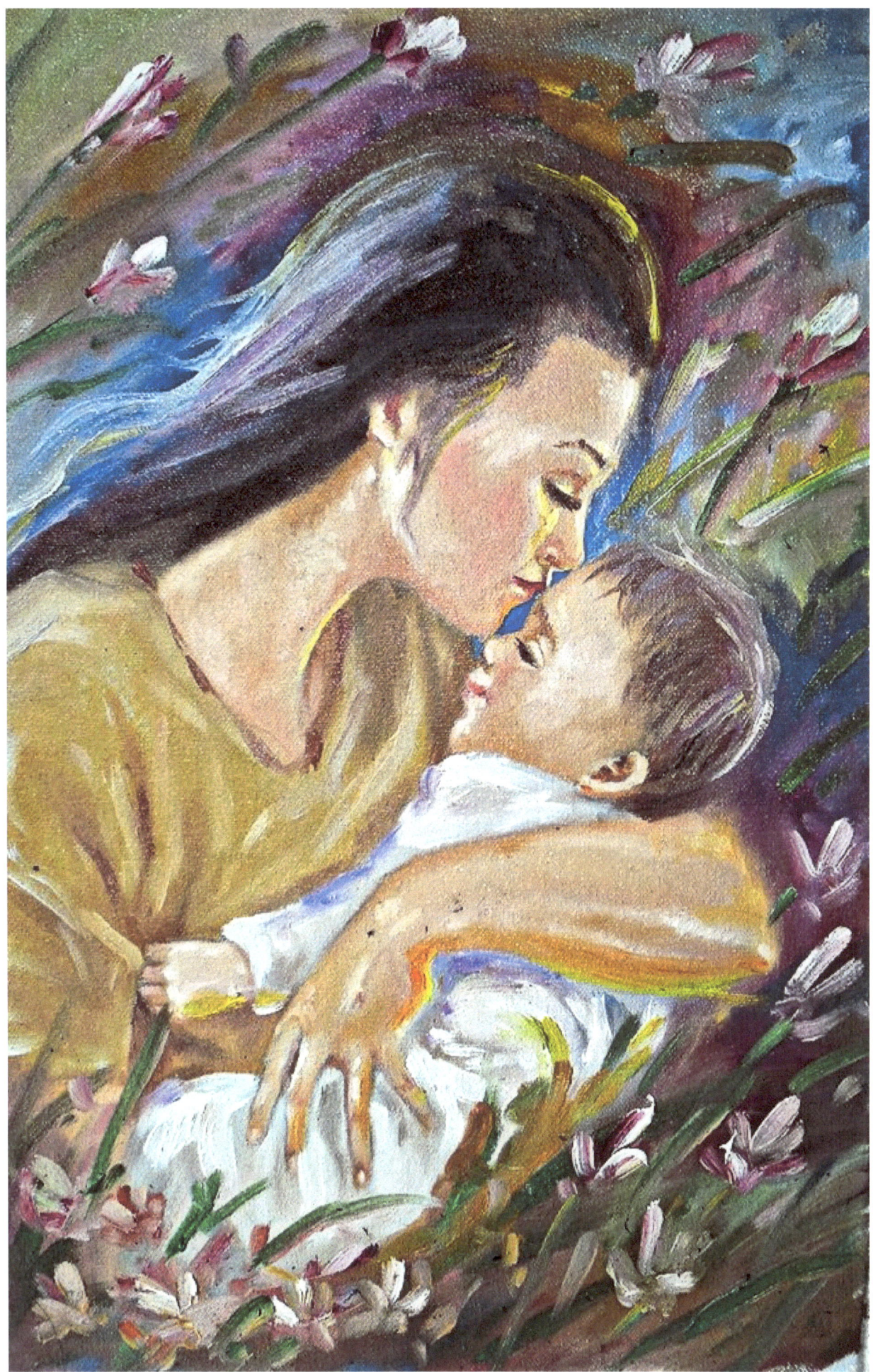

Joeyboi Galang - First Kiss, 12x16 in. Oil

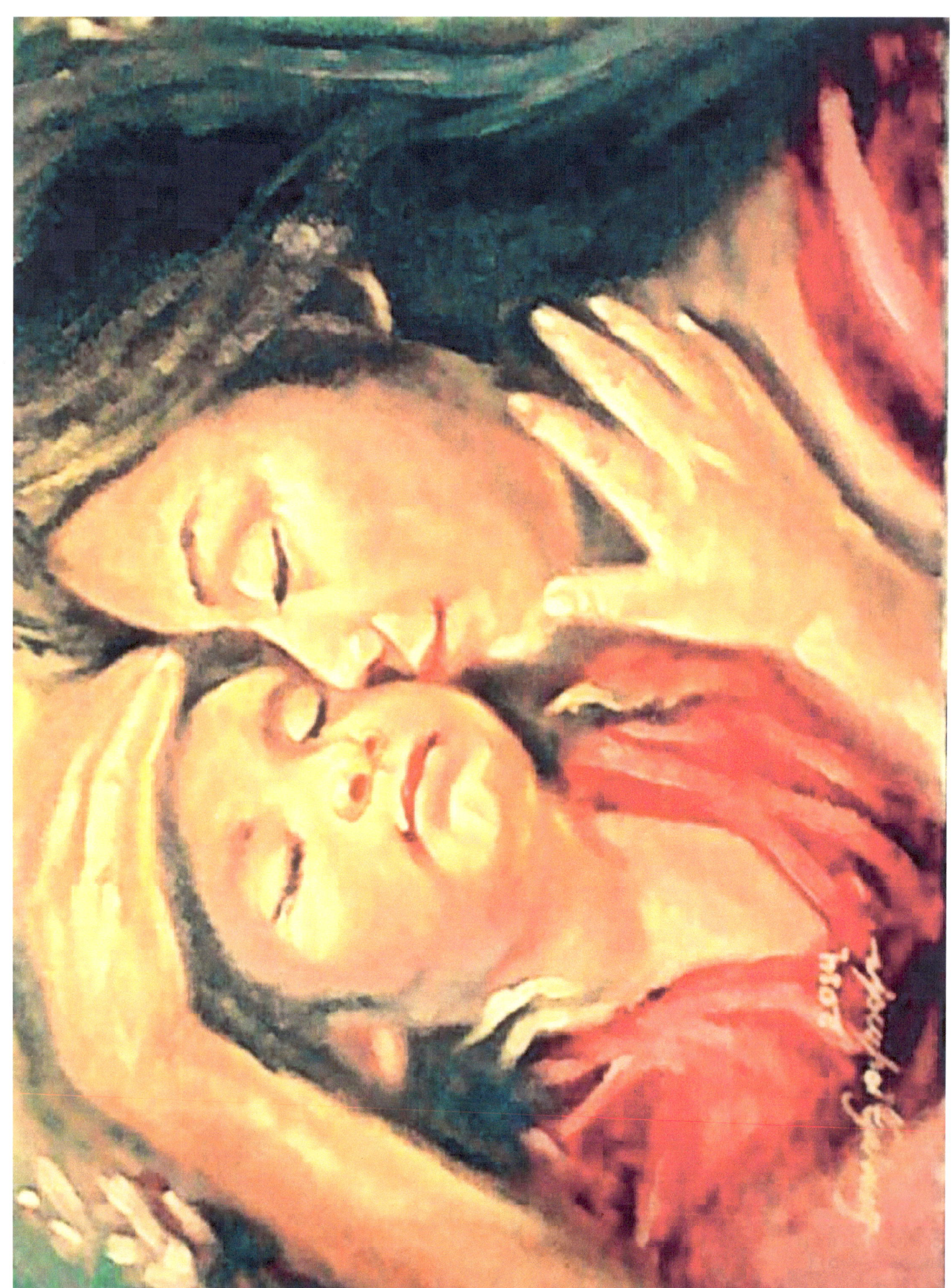

Joeyboi Galang - Mom-ents, 12x16 Oil

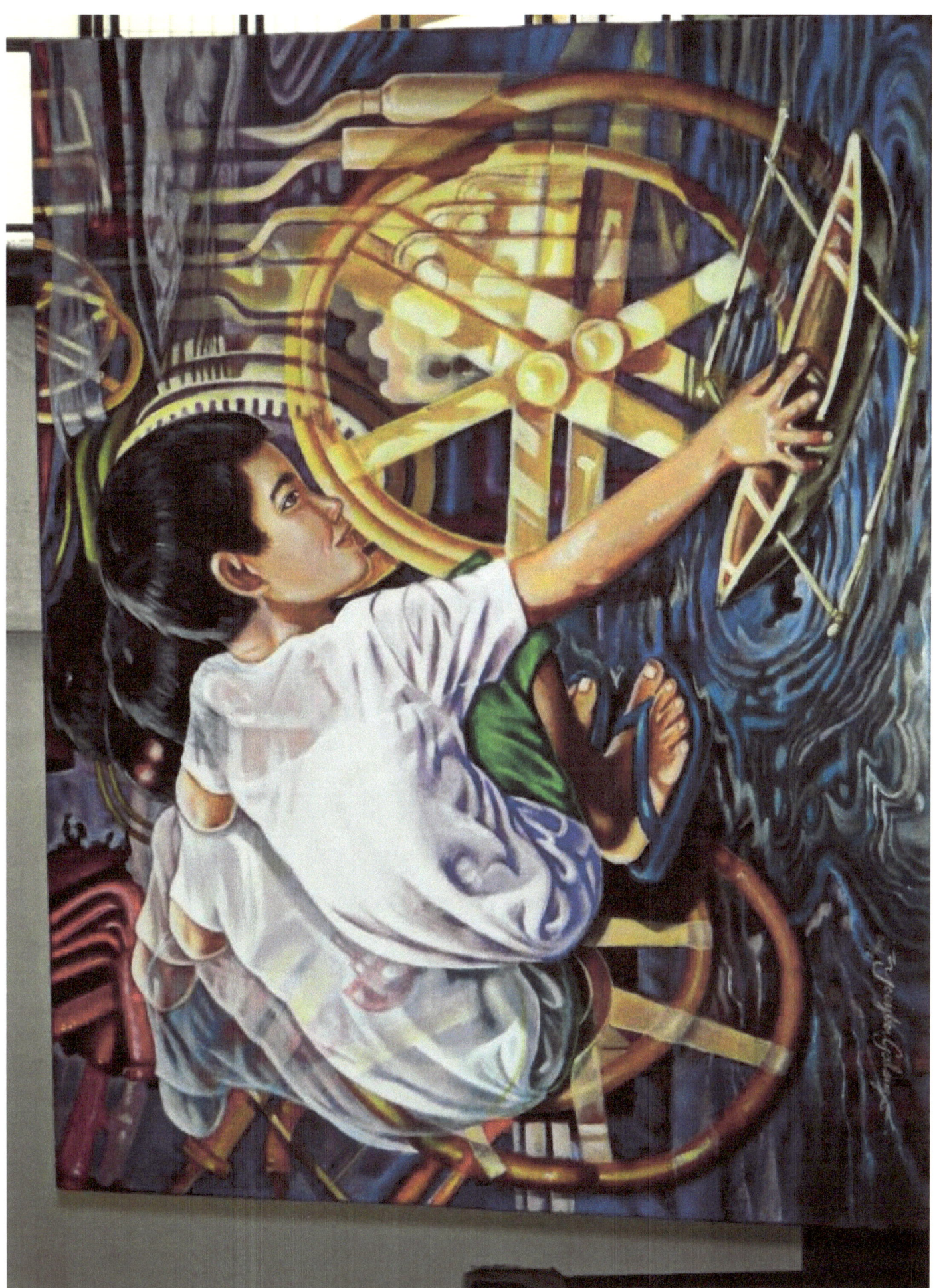

Joeyboi Galang - Unang Hakbang ni Kapitan Juan

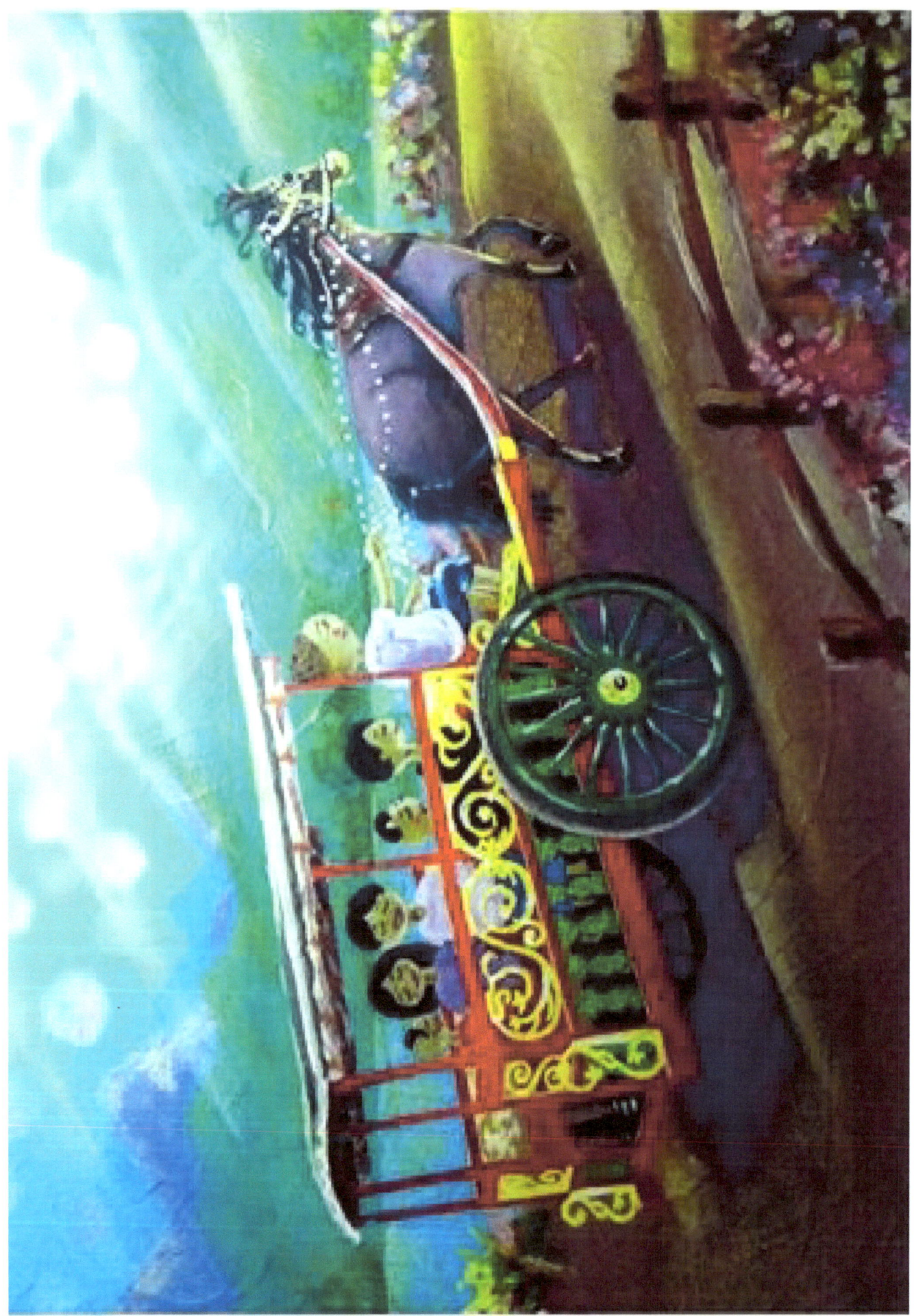

Joeyboi Galang - Destination Relaxation, 18x24 in. Acrylic

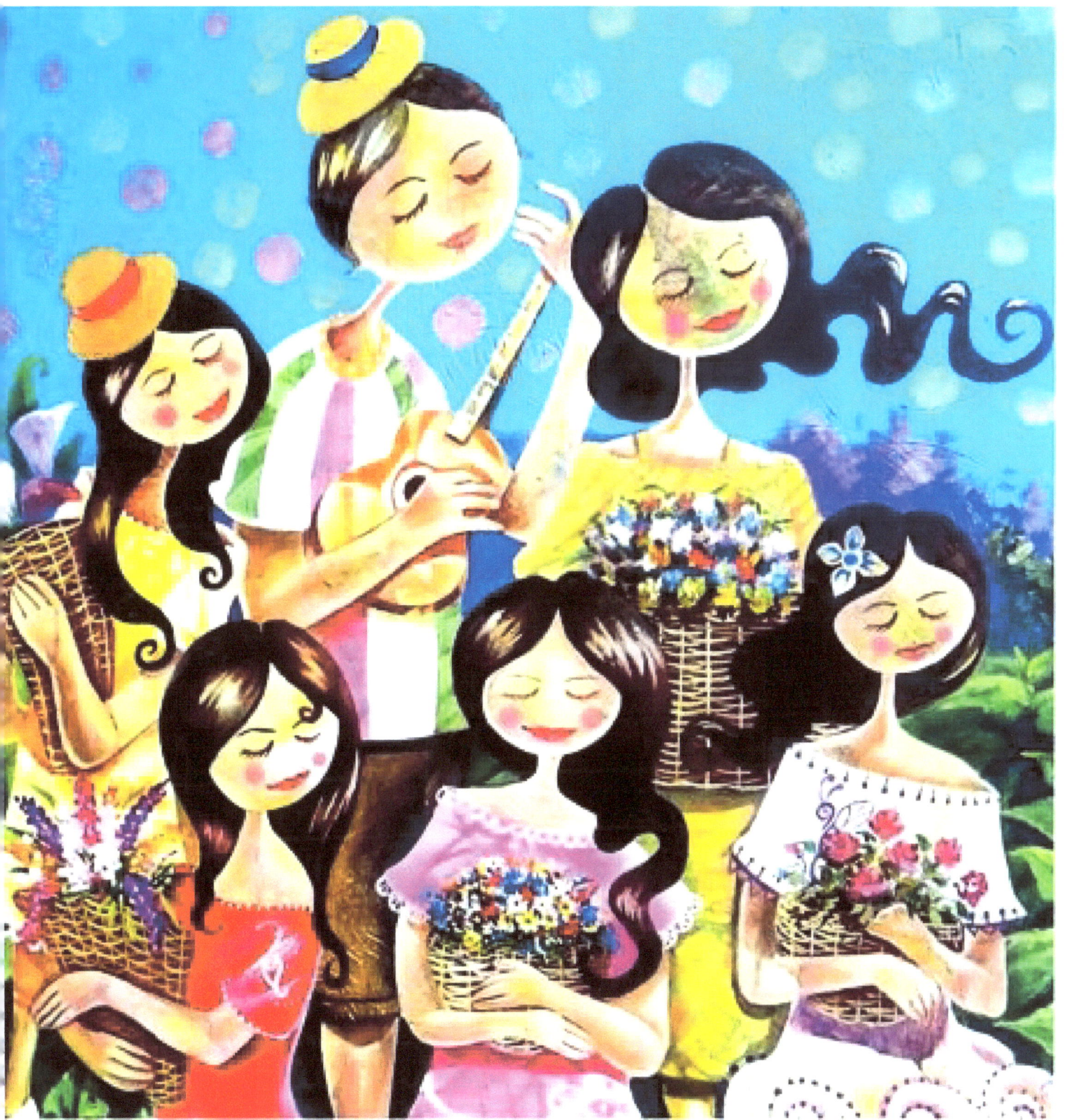

Joeyboi Galang - Family Bound By Love, 30x30 in. Acrylic

WELCOME! We hope you will enjoy this Art Gallery Book of collection of paintings and artwork by JOEYBOI GALANG. His actual paintings are available in Philippines and can be ordered in person or by mail or online. He can accept commission works. He can be contacted thru his facebook account under his name. Meanwhile, this book is size 8.5x11 inches. Each page is a paper print of his paintings and can cut out and framed separately, suitable for wall decor. The whole book is suitable as coffee table book for display in your living room and perfect as conversation piece.

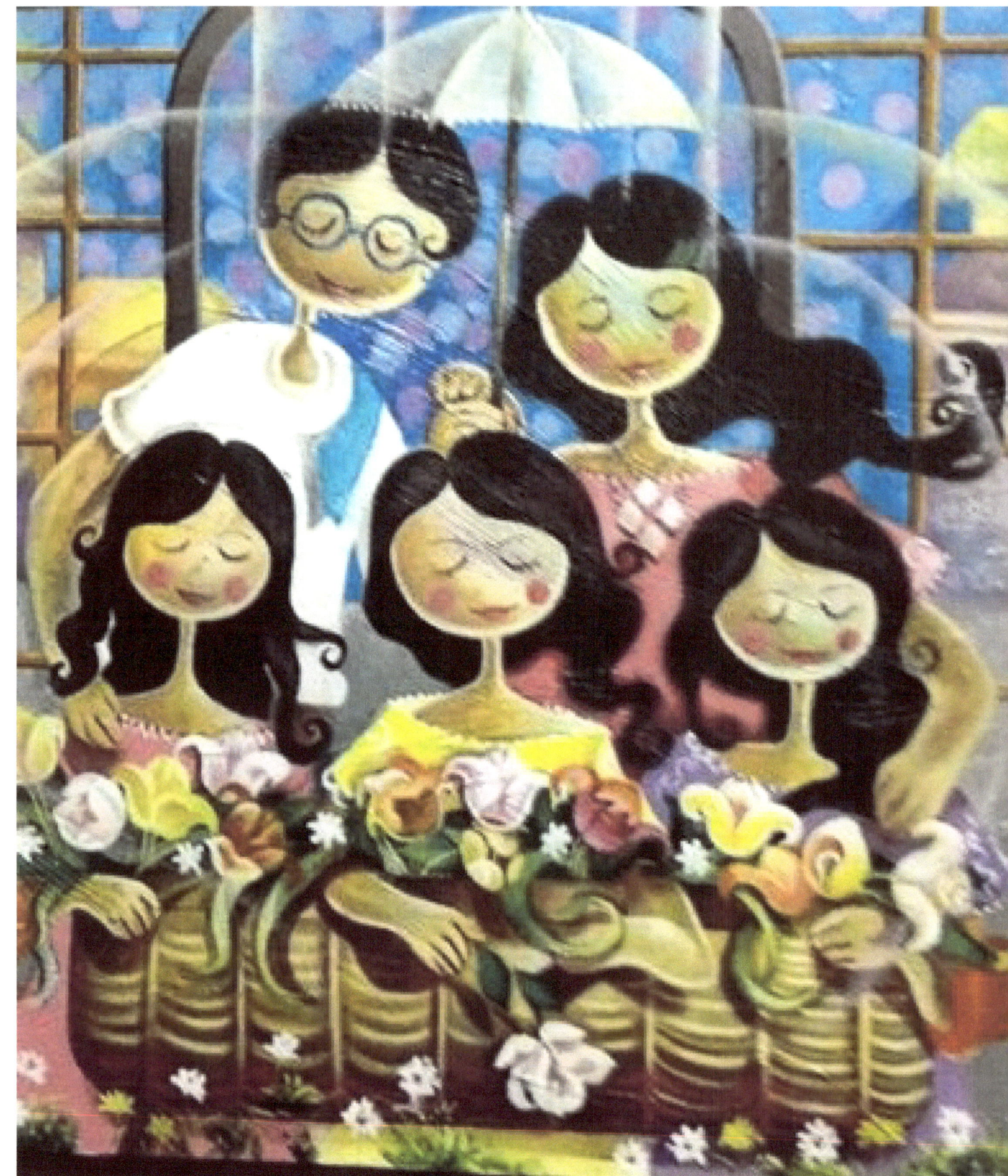

Joeyboi Galang - Family, Acrylic

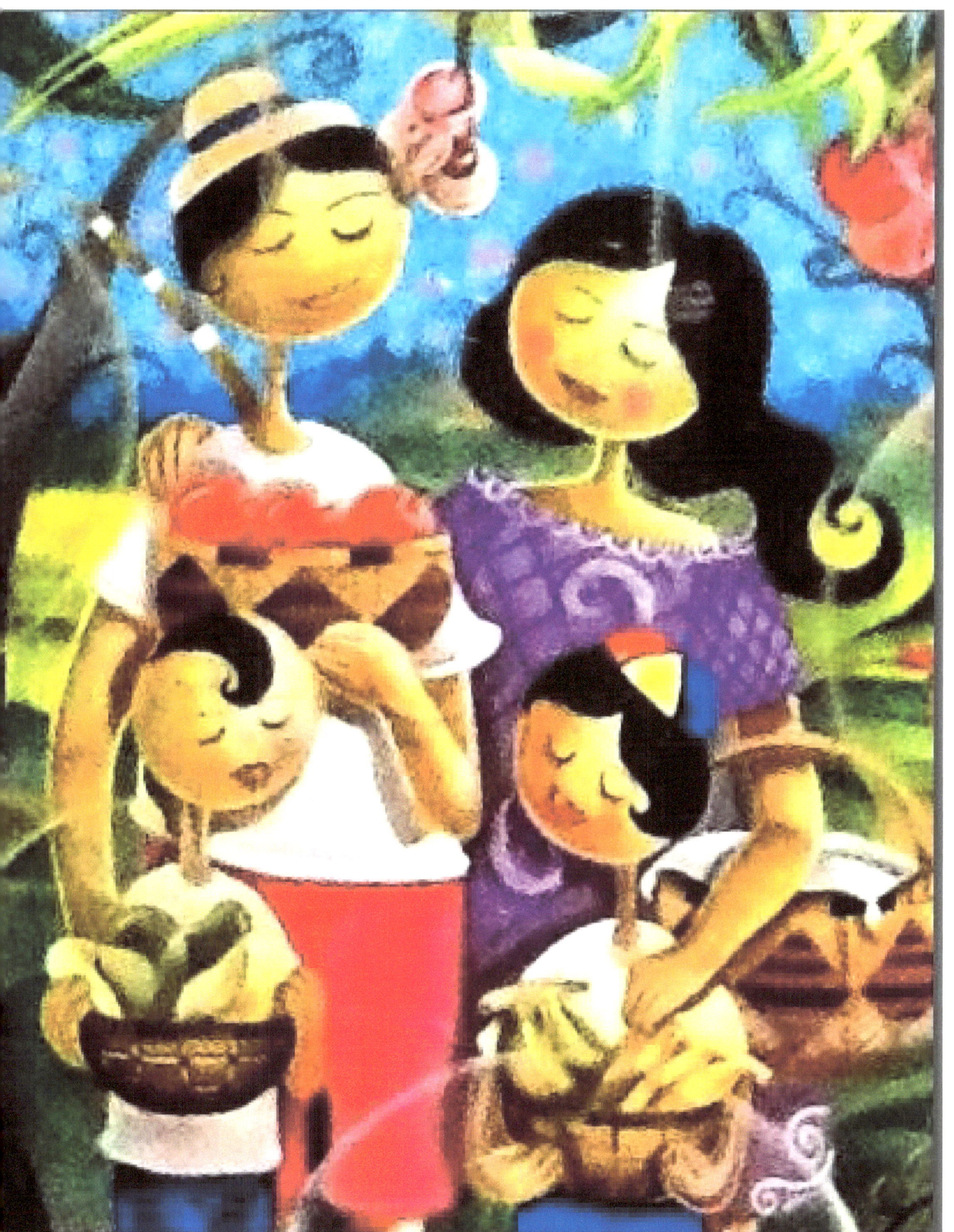

Joeyboi Galang - Family, Acrylic

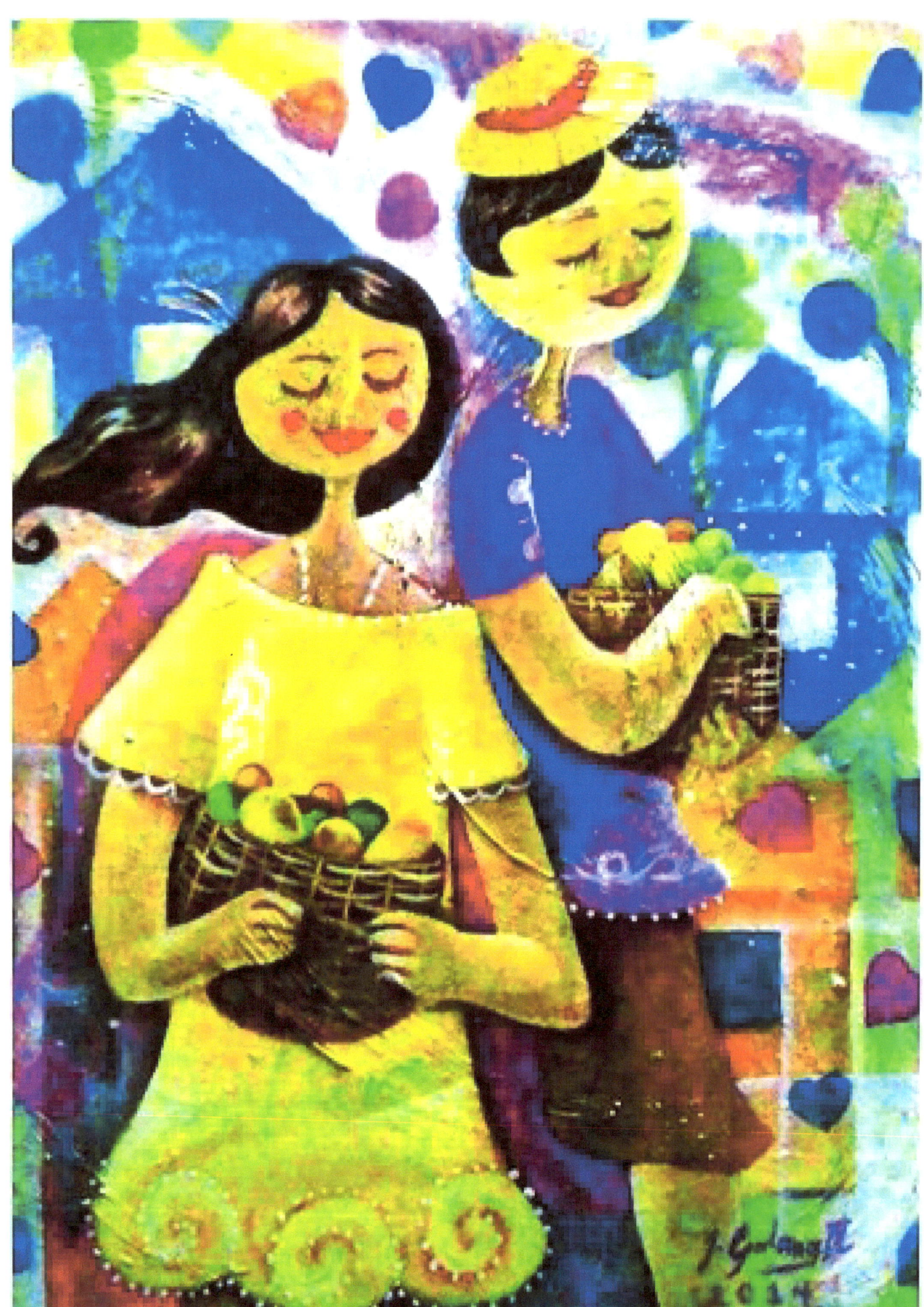

Joeyboi Galang - Fruits for Everyone, Acrylic

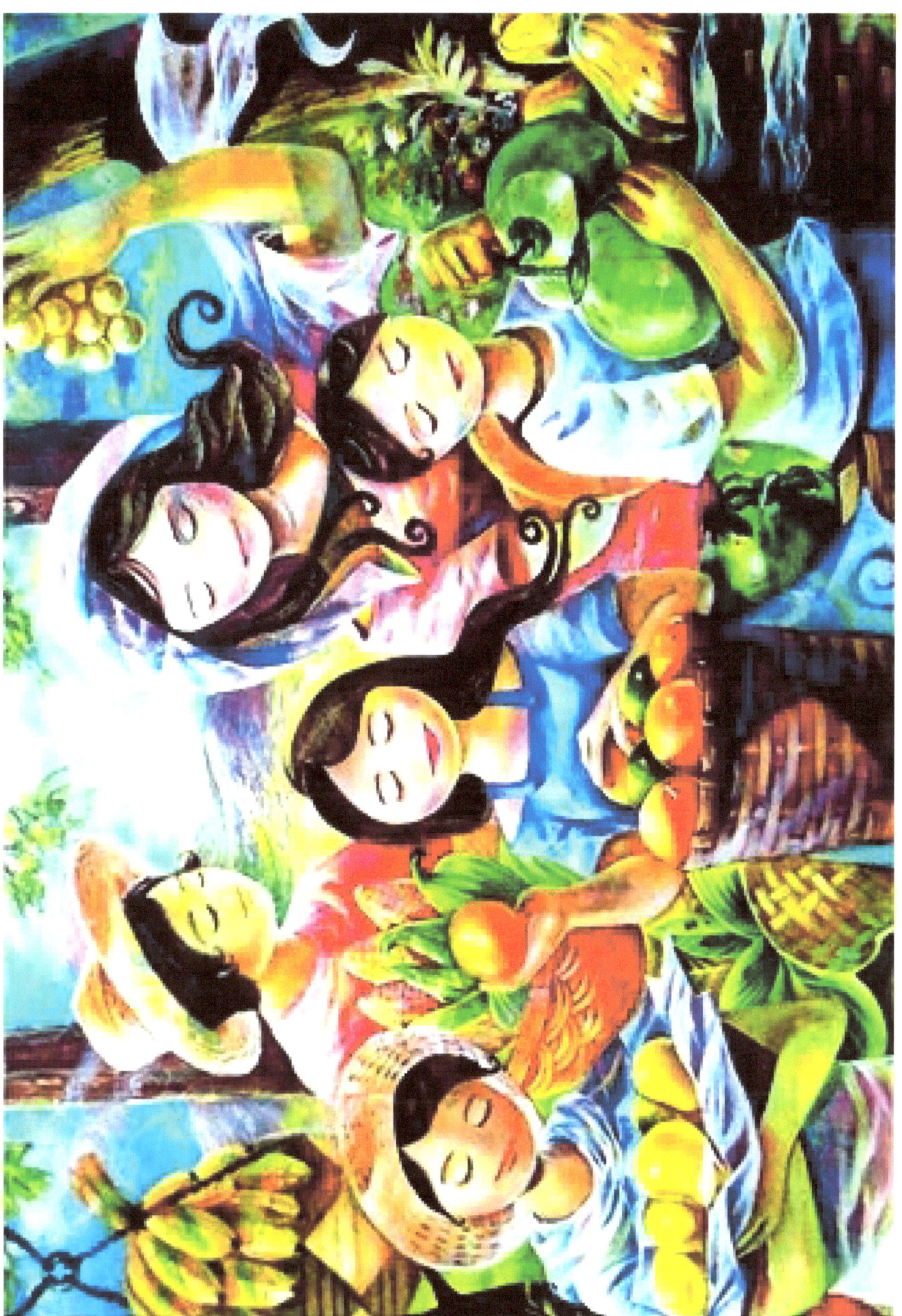

Joeyboi Galang - Family, Acrylic

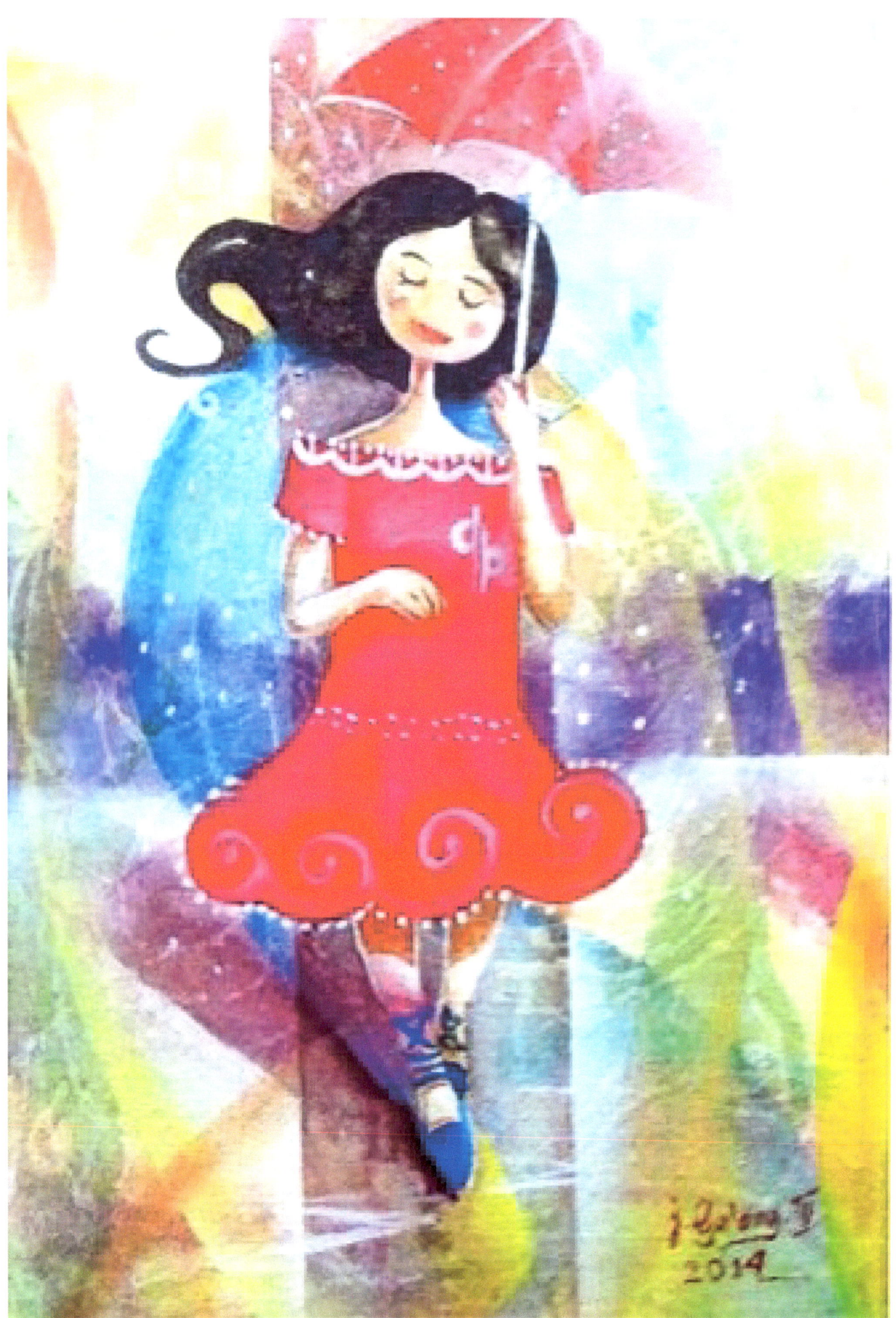

Joeyboi Galang - Girl with Umbrella, Acrylic

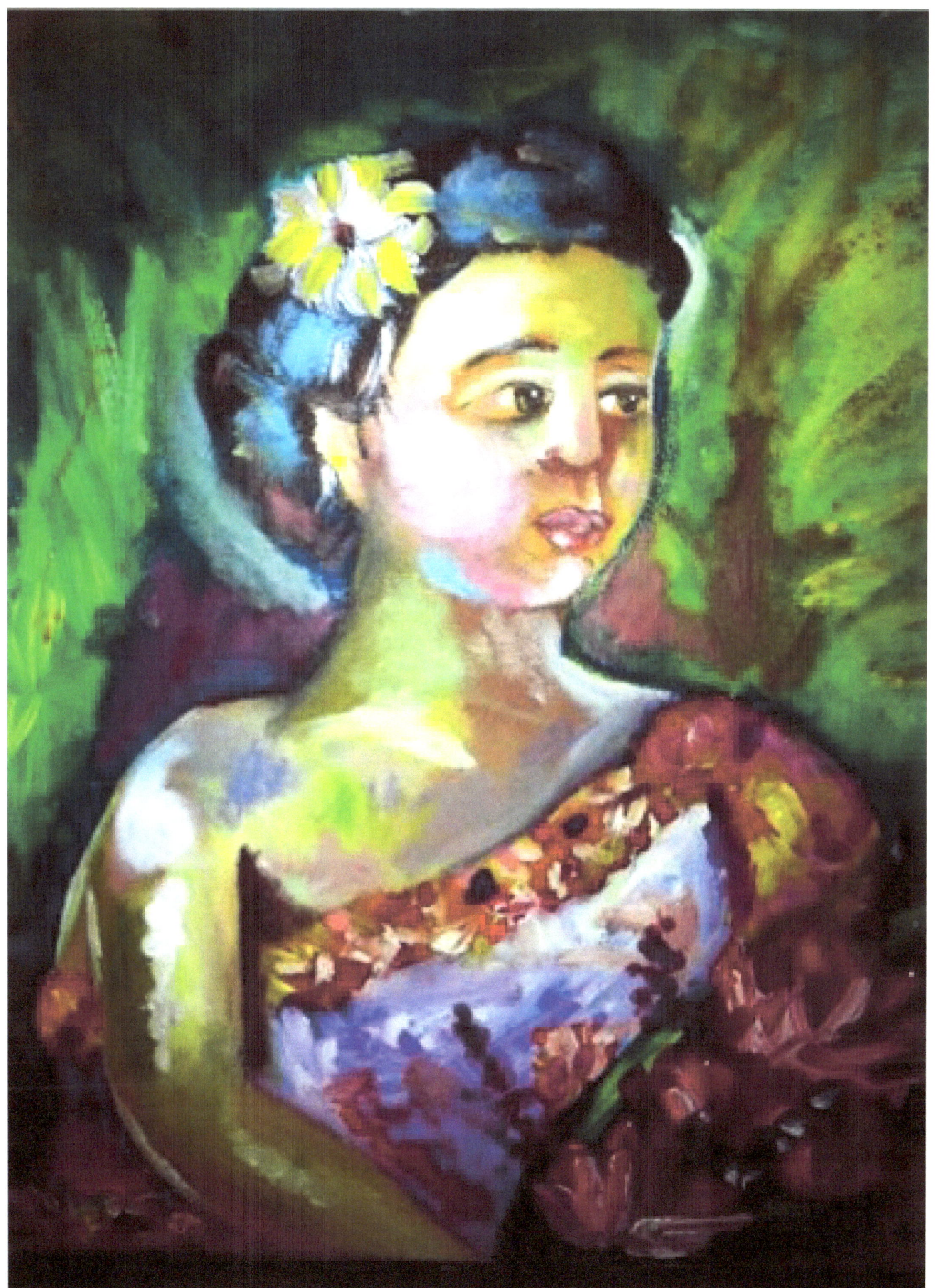

Joeyboi Galang - Young Girl, Acrylic

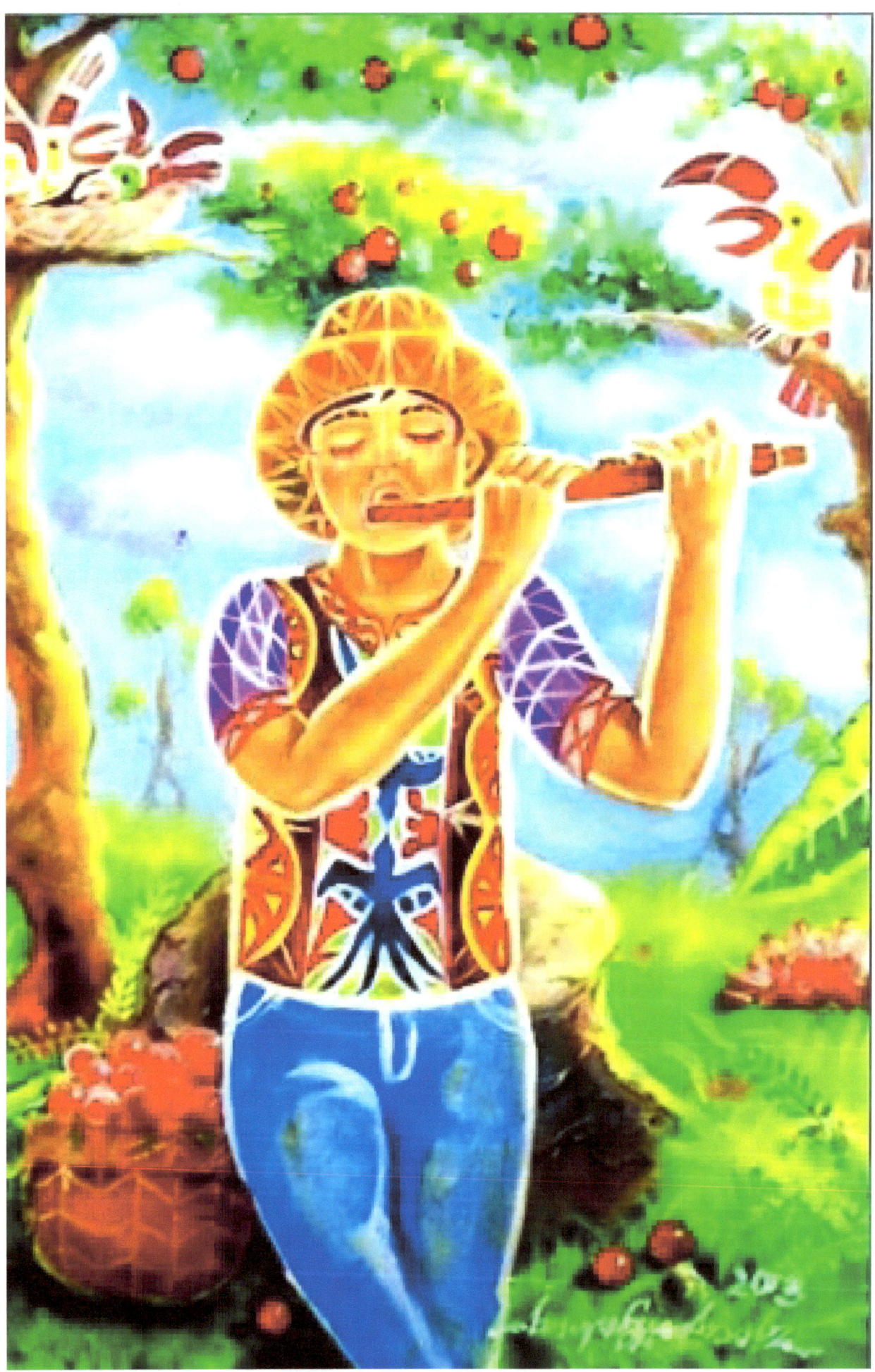

Joeyboi Galang - The Flutist, Acrylic

www.ingramcontent.com/pod-product-compliance
Lightning Source LLC
Chambersburg PA
CBHW050356180526

45159CB00005B/2039